NAVMC 26 10-AH

U.S. MARINE CORPS

"Force in Readiness"

LAY LEADER'S HANDBOOK

"Render to Caesar the things
that are Caesar's, and to
God the things that are God's."

St. Mark 12:17

FOREWORD

With the advent of new concepts of warfare
employed by the Marine Corps, trained Lay
Leaders are in a position to render signi-
ficant spiritual support to their brother
Marines.

Reliance upon the deep spirituality of religious minded Marines has been evident throughout our history. It was so on the Pacific
beaches in WWII and in Korea. It is now and
may be so any day in the future, for after all
we are a "Force In Readiness" and spiritual
readiness is as necessary as any other element
of the readiness we pride ourselves in.

This Lay Leader's Handbook then, is a part
of our equipment for mount-out and combat
use and demonstrates the traditional Marine
Corps concern for the total man.

WALLACE M. GREENE, JR.
General, U. S. Marine Corps
Commandant of the Marine Corps

PREFACE

This Lay Leader's Handbook is a revision of a manual first published in the 1st Marine Division in August, 1961. It represented the cooperative efforts of four chaplains: Chaplain David Plank, Assembly of God; Chaplain F. J. Murray, Catholic; Chaplain Howard Kummer, Jewish; and Chaplain Robert F. McComas, the then Division Chaplain.

In 1964, Chaplain Joseph H. Ryan revised and expanded the Catholic section and Chaplain A. G. Seniavsky added the Orthodox section. Other minor changes have been made since the 1961 edition and in connection with this present edition published at Headquarters, United States Marine Corps.

As Chaplain McComas said of this manual, "The book is a tool--a mere aid. What will make it useful will be to place it in the hands of a layman who loves God, his country and his fellow Marines and who will, after being appointed, prepare himself through prayer, worship, study and the cultivation of those habits which are the mark of a real man. To his hands this tool becomes a veritable instrument of power, not alone his, but also of God's.

"Spiritual power must be a recognized, respected, and carefully cultivated part of the power of our mighty 'Force in Readiness.' Without the help of a thousand laymen who are ready to stand up and be counted as men of God and who are willing to buckle down and work as servants of God in addition to being combat ready Marines, the lay leader program will fail.

There is no question of having the backing of Command leadership and the chaplains who serve with Marines. We need the force and power that dedicated laymen can give. We believe this manual can help toward that attainment.

We are grateful to Chaplain McComas and his associates in the Chaplain Corps who have produced this work and given their blessing to its further use.

L. M. LINDQUIST
CAPTAIN, CHC, USN
Staff Chaplain
Headquarters, U. S. Marine Corps

FOR GOD AND COUNTRY

GySgt E. R. WOJCIECHOWSKI, USMC

WORSHIP

O come, Let us worship and bow down;
Let us kneel before the Lord our Maker:
For He is our God,
And we are the people of His pasture,
And the sheep of His hand.

Psalm 95

Lord, what a change within us one short
   hour
Spent in Thy presence will prevail to
   make!
What heavy burdens from our bosoms
   take,
What parched grounds refresh as with a
   shower!
We kneel, and all around us seems to
   lower;
We rise, and all, the distant and the
   near,
Stands forth in sunny outline, brave and
   clear;
We kneel, how weak; we rise, how full
   of power!
Why, therefore, should we do ourselves
   this wrong,
Or others, that we are not always strong,
That we are ever overborne with care
That we should ever weak or heartless
   be,
Anxious or troubled, when with us is
   prayer,
And joy and strength and courage are
   with Thee!

-ARCHBISHOP TRENCH

WORSHIP

Two of the most fundamental and distinctive parts of a man are his spirit and his conscience. The spirit is nourished and the conscience sustained and sharpened by reverence- that activity of the spirit which declares and affirms the worth and glory of God.

We praise God and yet He needs not our praises. It is we who need to know and feel the closeness of God's presence, that He is our strength, a real power working in us the miracle not only of life, in the sense of being viable- being able to sit up and take nourishment- but of life abundant and eternal- being able to live meaningfully- coming to terms with life as we know it ought to be lived.

Life has consistently demonstrated that if a man does not worship God he worships something else or someone which time proves to be unworthy of standing in God's place.

The combination of worshipping the self and those things which gratify the self, produce an unwarranted confidence in the self to meet the demands of life which answers to the name of "sin" however well disguised.

It is sin because it is unalterably opposed to God, His purposes and our own best interests as individuals and as men in communion and collision with one another.

Only the worship of God, recognized at once as omnipotent, omniscient and the embodiment of all that is Love can make one alive to life and alert to claim all it has to offer a real man.

Worship helps us "see life steadily and see it whole" because we know God and give Him honor above all else.

Some things are so important we must learn them no matter what else has to be left undone. Chief among these is to know that "The Lord He is God; it is He that hath made us, and not we ourselves. We are His people, and the sheep of His pasture" and that "The Lord is nigh unto all them that call upon Him in Truth".

O come to the altar of God and worship.   Bow down your
    heads in reverence and pray.   Open your heart. . . Let
    him heal your sorrows . . Let your forebodings cease

Let him share with You the thunder and lightning of his
    mighty dream,
That you may rise in glad, good partnership to bring the
    world to him.

                    ROBERT F. McCOMAS

THE MARINE'S PRAYER

Almighty Father, whose command is over all and whose love never faileth; let me be aware of Thy presence and obedient to Thy will. Keep me true to my best self, guarding me against dishonesty in purpose and deed, and helping me so to live that I can stand unashamed and unafraid before my fellow Marines, my loved ones and Thee. Protect those in whose love I live, give me the will to do the work of a Marine and to accept my share of responsibilities with vigor and enthusiasm. Grant me fortitude that I may be proficient in my daily performance. Keep me loyal and faithful to my superior officers; make me considerate of those entrusted to my leadership and faithful to the duties my country and the Marine Corps has entrusted to me. Help me always to wear my uniform with dignity, and let it remind me daily of the traditions of the service of which I am a part. If I am inclined to doubt, steady my faith; if I am tempted, make me strong to resist; if I should miss the mark, give me courage to try again. Guide me with the light of truth and grant me wisdom by which I may understand the answer to my prayer.

Amen.

TABLE OF CONTENTS

SECTION I

THE AUTHORIZATION AND BACKGROUND OF

THE LAY LEADER

According to Navy Regulations, the commanding officer is ultimately responsible for the observance of Sunday and the conduct of divine services. It is the chaplain's duty to actually perform those duties relating to the religious activities of the command, including the conduct of divine services. It is also the commanding officer's responsibility and the chaplain's duty to arrange for the conduct of divine services in the unit when a chaplain is not available.

Within this framework, then, and in view of the fact that most all religious groups permit laymen to conduct some form of public religious worship or devotion in the absence of their ordained clergy, the commanding officer is authorized to delegate lay leaders to assist in the religious program and to conduct divine services. BUPERS INSTRUCTIONS 1730 series, the Marine Corps Manual, paragraph 1730 and the Marine SOP's for Chaplain Service in the various Commands specifically authorize the Lay Leader Program and outline the particulars thereto.

SECTION II

THE CHARACTER AND MISSION OF THE LAY LEADER

A religious lay leader is a non-ordained person whose privilege and task It is to assist his Command and the chaplain in religious ministrations. And in the chaplain's absence, yet under his supervision, to carry out certain functions which pertain to divine worship and the unit's overall religious program. You have been carefully selected and duly appointed to perform this important volunteer duty.

Thus in your position as lay leader, you represent not just the chaplain or the Command's religious program; you directly represent Almighty God. He who desires to be an excellent lay leader will strive for excellence in the area of personal piety, public and private conduct, and the spoken word.

If you succeed, men will come closer to God because of you. If you fail, they will drift further from Him. Make "excellence for God" your constant aim and effort.

SECTION III

THE TASKS OF THE LAY LEADERS

The following paragraphs define the tasks and limits of the
lay leader:

     1. Conduct as appropriate, service of worship or de-
votion. Refrain from formal preaching, specialized counsel-
ling, administration of the sacraments, and any other activities which presume ordination by a religious body. An of-
fering will not be taken at a lay-led service. The chaplain
will provide materials for sermons as needed.

     2. In the field and/or in combat situations, the lay
leader may assist the wounded or dying, distribute chaplain-
approved literature, conduct appropriate services, and carry
out such other religious functions as may he delegated and
approved by the commanding officer or chaplain.

     3. In garrison, the lay leader will publicize the chap-
el and religious program, encourage attendance at divine
services both by word of mouth and by personal example.
refer men to the chaplain who may need his help, and assist in the unit's overall religious program in such other
ways as may be requested and deemed appropriate by the
commanding officer or chaplain.

     4. The lay leader who has conducted worship services,
devotionals, ministered to the wounded and dying or conducted any other noteworthy ministry, should report same just
as soon as possible to his chaplain, or a supervisory chaplain if appropriate.

SECTION IV

THE EQUIPMENT OF THE LAY LEADER

The equipment which you will bring to your tasks is twofold:
personal and physical. First of all you must be spiritually equipped to fulfill the religious ministry which is yours.
Personal piety as cultivated by private religious devotions.
public worship, and a morally disciplined life will best equip
you to perform your important duties. The man who is not
so equipped but is bankrupt therein, will only be of disser-
vice to those whom he has been commissioned to serve.

Secondly, there are certain items of physical equipment which you will need. As a Marine, you will have little room in your pack or carrying anything other than essentials. Hence the items shown are minimal. Your chaplain will advise you as to the quantities you should maintain. Your equipment will be supplied by either your unit chaplain, or in some cases, by the supervisory chaplain.

1. CATHOLIC:

    a. Crucifix: The chaplain may be able to supply you with one for the conduct of divine services.

    b. Rosaries and medals (blessed)

    c. Father Stedman's "My Sunday Missal"

    d. Father Peyton's "Rosary Prayer Book"

    e. Small Hymnal, such as "Song and Service Book for Ship and Field"

    f. New Testament

2. PROTESTANT:

    a. Cross: If you do not have one, or the chaplain is not able to supply you with a cross, you may construct one from two suitable lengths of "nod or tree limbs.

    b. New Testaments

    c. Hymnals as above, or hymn sheets

    d. Order of worship folders

    e. Devotional guide such as "Upper Room" or "Family Altar"

3. JEWISH:

    a. "Selected Jewish Songs for Members of the Armed Forces"

    b. "Prayer Book for Jewish Personnel In the Armed Forces of the United States"

    c. Prayer shawl (palis)

4. <u>ORTHODOX</u>:

    a. One pair candle holders

    b. One Crucifix with Corpus

    c. One Bible, King James Version

    d. Eastern Orthodox Prayer Books

5. <u>OTHER FAITHS</u>:

    See a chaplain.

In addition to the above, your chaplain will periodically supply you with other items which will be helpful to you. If you have, or know of materials oilier than those shown above which you desire to utilize, secure first the approval of the chaplain before using them. Also, the chaplain may supply you in quantity with items such as tracts and devotional booklets which you may distribute to those who need or request them.

SECTION V

THE PREPARATION OF THE LAY LEADER

Probably the most important duty which has been delegated to you is the conduct of divine services. Ordinarily you will conduct such services only when you are away from garrison, out on a training exercise, and a chaplain is onavailable. Neither you nor the chaplain may know far ahead of time whether or not it will become your task to hold services. For it may be only at the last minute on Sunday that the chaplain, who has planned to be present, is unable to reach your unit for some reason. Thus the conduct of services will be solely up to you.

Hence, every lay leader must make preparation to conduct divine services prior to departing for the field. It would also be well to assume that any and all equipment which you may need in this regard will be unobtainable once you have left garrison. Thus you must take with you to the field everything you may need. Following is the very minimum equipment which the lay leader should have with him in the field.

CATHOLIC:

Copies of "My Sunday Missal"; quantities of rosaries, the Lay Leader Manual; and other helps for which you may have room.

PROTESTANT:

Copies of "Song and Service Book", other appropriate hymnals, or printed hymn sheets; the Lay Leader Manual; and other helps for which you may have room.

JEWISH:

Prayer shawl; copies of "Selected Jewish Songs" and copies of "Prayer Book Abridged for Jewish Personnel."

ORTHODOX:

a. One pair candle holders

b. One Crucifix with Corpus

c. One Bible, King James Version

d. Eastern Orthodox Prayer Books

Once you are in the field, arid it appears that you will be conducting either Sunday or midweek divine services, discuss the subject with your unit Executive Officer (or the Executive Officer of the ship upon which you may be embarked), and ascertain the best time and place for them to be held. The time chosen should conflict as little as possible with the problem or exercise that may be in progress, and it should be so set that a maximum number of men can attend. Thus your service may be scheduled for 0700, 1400, or 2000.

Next you must decide upon a suitable place to hold the service. Select a spot that will accommodate at least twenty-five men, and that will allow them to comfortably kneel. It may be under a tree, in a draw, on a hillside, or on a ship's fantail. Tidy up the area if necessary, and plan to locate yourself as the leader near the altar (if you have one) so that you and the symbols of worship can be seen by the worshippers.

Rigging for services comes next. If you are fortunate enough to have a cross, or if you have constructed one, you may wish to set up an altar on a jeep's hood, stacked ammunition cases, or some other raised flat surface. Any efforts which you expend in rigging for church; in creating an atmosphere, or even a suggestion of worship; or in providing any symbols, facilities, or decorations which will produce a set-apart place inducing a spirit of reverence, will be much appreciated by those who worship and will bring greater glory to Cod.

Once the time and place have been selected, take steps to see that the word is passed announcing services at least forty-five minutes prior to the appointed time. The announcement might read like this: "Protestant (Catholic) Divine Services will be held at 0900, in the draw behind the Company CP." It can be promulgated in several ways: (1) get about yourself, passing the word to as many as you can contact, especially to key men such as platoon and section leaders, who in turn will pass the word to the men under them; (2) utilize any radio and communications facilities which may be available for reaching remotely located personnel; and (3) write or type or mimeograph the announcement, hand out individually, and post in conspicuous places such as in or near the chow area. (Note: Make certain that you secure permission, as may be appropriate, to pass the word as suggested above.)

Now that the time and place have been arranged and an-Nounced, and rigging for church has been completed, all should be in readiness for the service to begin. Certainly by this time you should completely be familiar with the parts of the service and their order. You should have made at least one "dry run" through the entire service, rehearsing the whole and each of its parts for smoothness, the transmittal of meaning and understanding, and the creation of an attitude of worship: becoming familiar with the correct pronounciation and meaning of strange words which may appear in the scripture reading for instance; making the prayers reverent and devotional expressions from your own heart, not mere words to be read monotonously by rote; and finally, bringing yourself to that devout attitude of soul and mind which will best fit and enable you to lead others in their worship of Cod.

If you have prepared carefully and faithfully in the ways described above, God will indeed be glorified and worshipped; the worshippers will be edified, inspired, and strengthened and you will be rewarded in ways too sacred to describe and too numerous to count.

SECTION VI

THE TRAINING OF THE LAY LEADER

The training which you as a lay leader will receive is two-fold: self-training, and the training which will be given by the chaplain.

As a lay leader you have the responsibility to use every means at your disposal to prepare and train yourself to the best of your ability to carry out your lay-leader responsibilities. This involves faithful fulfillment of all your religious obligations; faithful performance of private devotional exercises; setting a good example among your mates in word and deed; and becoming easily familiar with all your lay-leader duties, including the conduct of divine services and the materials used in their performance.

The second type of training is that which is administered by the chaplain. Besides the personal training, guidance, and assistance which he will give you, Lay Leader Conferences will be conducted periodically. Here the chaplain by group instruction will seek to train and equip you and your fellow Lay leaders for the effective performance of your important duties.

SECTION VII

THE PROTESTANT LAY LEADER SERVICE

"To worship God is to quicken the conscience by the holiness of God, to feed the mind with the truth of God, to purge the imagination by the beauty of God, to open the heart to the love of God, and to devote the will to the purpose of God."

-by William Temple

The above lines aptly summarize that which transpires within a person who worships God in spirit and in truth. When

7

we thus worship, we honor, reverence, and pay homage to
God in a way which pleases Him, and which he expects of
us His children. The worshipper arises spiritually nourished
and in newness of life, freshly fitted and strengthened to meet
his responsibilities and duties. It is your privilege and ob-
ligation to conduct just such a service of worship.

Worship may be either private, between the individual and
God, or it may be public, taking place in the company of
others. It is your task to lead a group of Marines in a service of public worship, that together you might render your
hearts devotion to God and receive His blessings.

In deciding on the manner in which you will conduct the worship service, you must first take into consideration the fact
that a variety of church denominations will be represented in
your congregation. Some men may be Baptist or Nazarene,
accustomed to a more or less "free" worship service; others
may be Lutheran or Episcopal, and will prefer to worship in
a more formally, or liturgically, conducted service. Hence
you most be discreet in choosing a form of worship which
will satisfy the devotional needs of your denominationally-
mixed congregation, not offend their religious sensibilities,
and yet not be contrary to the dictates of your own conscience
and church.

To assist you toward this end, the following order of worship is suggested. It includes these essentials of a true
worship experience; the adoration of God, the confession of
sin, an affirmation of Christian faith, and a dedication of
life. Therefore, regardless of how short or simple your
service may be, it must include those expressions of worship
which permit the worshippers to fulfill each one of these essentials in one or more ways. Here is a suggested order of
worship which embodies these essential elements:

1.   The Adoration Of God

A.   A Call To Worship (lay leader)

B.   A Hymn of Adoration and Praise

C.   A Prayer of Invocation (lay leader)

2.   The Confession Of Sin

D.   A Prayer of General Confession (in unison) or a period
     of silent prayer for individual confession

E.   A Prayer For Pardon

F.   The Lord's Prayer (in unison) followed by a Scriptural
     Assurance of Pardon

3.   <u>The Affirmation Of Faith</u>

G.   Special Music

H.   A Responsive Reading

I.   The Creed or Affirmation Of Faith (in unison)

J.   The Scripture Lesson (lay leader)

K.   A Prayer Of Thanksgiving and Supplication (lay leader)

4.   <u>The Dedication Of Life</u>

L.   A Hymn of Preparation

W.   The Message (lay leader)

N.   A Hymn of Dedication

O.   A Closing Prayer (lay leader)

NOTE: The headings of the four sections which appear above
        are not to be announced or referred to during the
        service. They are merely included here to indicate
        to you how the various parts of the service can con-
        tribute to one complete, unified worship experience.

For a Sunday morning worship service you will no doubt wish
to follow the above order of worship just as it is shown.
However, it may be that for a simpler midweek evening devotional service you may desire to follow an order of worship shorter than this. In that case you may choose one or
more elements from each of the four sections, thus still including the essentials of Adoration, Confession, Affirmation,
and Dedication. Such a brief service might look like this:

        A.   A Call To Worship

        B.   A Hymn of Adoration and Praise

        D.   A Prayer of Confession, or Period of
             Silence for Individual Confession

F. The Lord's Prayer

I. The Creed

J. The Scripture Lesson

N. A Hymn of Dedication

O. A Closing Prayer

Each element of the worship service will now he taken up in
its order:

A. <u>CALL TO WORSHIP</u>

The Call To Worship simply summons the congregation to
present themselves before God in humble worship. One of
the following scriptural calls may be used. Your chaplain
can suggest calls particularly appropriate for special days
and seasons of the Christian Year, such as Advent, Christ-
mas and Easter (the same holds true for the portions of the
service which follow, such as hymns, prayers, and scripture lessons).

(1) O come, let us worship and bow down, let us kneel
before the Lord our maker. For he is our God, and we are
the people of His pasture, and the sheep of His hand. Know
ye that the Lord he is God, it is He that hath made us and
not we ourselves.

(2) O come, let us sing unto the Lord, let us make a
joyful noise to the rock of our salvation. Let us come before his presence with thanksgiving and make a joyful noise
unto him with psalms. For the Lord is a great God, and a
great King above all gods.

(3) The Lord is in His holy temple, let all the earth keep
silence before Him. Rest in the Lord, wait patiently for Him
Cease from anger and forsake wrath, fret not thyself in any
wise to do evil, for evil doers shall be cut off, but those
that wait upon the Lord, they shall inherit the earth.

(4) Make a joyful noise unto the Lord, all the earth, rejoice and sing praises! Sing unto the Lord with the harp,
with the harp and the voice of a psalm. Let the sea roar
and the fullness thereof, the world and they that dwell therein. For He cometh to judge the earth. With righteousness
shall He judge the world and the people with equity.

B.   HYMNS OF ADORATION AND PRAISE

The hymns sung in the service may be introduced by you
with words much as these; "Let us now sing together 'Come
Thou Almighty King' which is found _____". Appropriate
hymns expressing adoration and praise to God, in addition to
those shown below, may be found in hymnals with which your
chaplain will supply you.

(1)   All Hail The Power of Jesus' Name

          All Hail the power of Jesus' name!
          Let angels prostrate fall;
          Bring forth the royal diadem,
          And crown Him Lord of all,
          Bring forth the royal diadem,
          And crown Him Lord of all.

          Ye seed of Israel's chosen race,
          Ye ransomed of the fall;
          Hail Him, who saves you by His grace,
          And crown Him Lord of all,
          Hail Him, who saves you by His grace,
          And crown Him Lord of all.

          Sinners, whose love can ne'er forget
          The wormwood and the gall
          Go spread your trophies at His feet,
          And crown Him Lord of all,
          Go spread your trophies at His feet,
          And crown Him Lord of all.

          Let every kindred, every tribe,
          On this terrestrial ball,
          To Him all majesty ascribe,
          And crown Him Lord of all,
          To Him all majesty ascribe,
          And crown Him Lord of all.

          O that with yonder sacred throng,
          We at His feet may fall;
          We'll join the everlasting song,
          And crown Him Lord of all,
          We'll join the everlasting song,
          And crown Him Lord of all.

(2)   Holy Holy Holy Lord God Almighty

Holy, Holy, Holy! Lord God Almighty!
Early in the morning our song shall rise to Thee;
Holy, holy, holy, merciful and mighty
God in three persons, blessed trinity!

Holy, holy, holy! all the saints adore Thee,
Casting down their golden crowns around the glassy
    sea;
Cherubim and seraphim falling down before Thee,
Which wert, and art, and evermore shalt be.

Holy, holy, holy! Tho' the darkness hide Thee,
Though the eyes of sinful man Thy glory may not see,
Only Thou art holy, there is none beside Thee,
Perfect in power, in love, and purity

Holy, holy, holy! Lord God Almighty
All Thy works shall praise Thy name, in earth, and
    sky, and sea;
Holy, holy, holy, merciful and mighty!
God in three persons, blessed Trinity! Amen.

(3)   O For A Thousand Tongues

O For a thousand tongues to sing
My great Redeemer's praise
The glories of my God and King,
The triumphs of His grace.

My gracious Master and my God,
Assist me to proclaim,
To spread through all the earth abroad,
The honors of Thy name.

Jesus! The name that charms our fears,
That bids our sorrows cease:
'Tis music in the sinner 5 ears,
'Tis life, and health, and peace.

He breaks the power of canceled sin,
He sets the prisoner free;
His blood can make the foulest clean
His blood availed for me.

Hear Him ye deaf; His praise, ye dumb,
Your loosened tongues employ;
Ye blind, behold your Saviour come;
And leap, ye lame for joy. Amen.

(4) Come Thou Almighty King

Come, Thou Almighty King, Help us thy name to sing,
Help us to praise; Father, all glorious
O'er all victorious, Come and reign over us
Ancient of Days.

Come, Thou incarnate word, Gird on Thy mighty
    sword,
Our prayer attend; Come, and Thy people bless,
And give Thy word success; Spirit of holiness,
On us descend.

Come, holy Comforter, Thy sacred witness bear
In this glad hour; Thou, who almighty art,
Now rule in every heart, and ne'er from us depart,
Spirit of power.

To the great One in Three Eternal praises be,
Hence evermore; His sovereign majesty
May we in glory see, and to eternity
Love and adore. Amen.

C. PRAYERS OF INVOCATION

In the Prayer Of Invocation we reverently call upon God to
meet with us in our act of worship, to hear our prayers, to
fill the needs of our heart, and to spiritually fit us to worthily worship Him. One of the following prayers may be
used. It, as well as the prayers which follow in the service,
should he preceded by the words, "Let Us Pray".

(1) Almighty God, unto whom all hearts are open, all desires known, and from whom no secrets are hid; cleanse the
thoughts of our hearts by the inspiration of thy Holy Spirit,
that we may perfectly love Thee, and worthily magnify Thy
Holy Name; through Christ our Lord. Amen.

(2) Almighty God, purify our hearts from every vain and
sinful thought; prepare our souls to worship Thee this day
acceptably, with reverence and godly fear. Set our affection
on things above, and give us grace to receive Thy word into
good and honest hearts, so that we may rise to newness of
life; through Jesus Christ our Lord. Amen.

(3) O God our Father, who hast bidden the light to shine
out of darkness, who hast again wakened us to praise Thy
goodness and ask for Thy grace; accept now the sacrifice of
our worship and thanksgiving. Make us to be children of the
light and of the day, and heirs of Thy everlasting inheritance.
Remember, O God, thy whole Church, all our brethren by
land or sea who stand in need of Thy grace. Pour out the
riches of Thy mercy, so that we, being redeemed, and steadfast in faith, may ever praise Thy wonderful and Holy Name;
through Jesus Christ our Lord. Amen.

(4) O God, to whom belong adoration and praise; prepare
us, through the active presence of thy Spirit, to come before
Thee worthily and to ask of Thee rightly; enlighten our understanding; purify our every desire; quicken our wills unto instant obedience to Thy word; strengthen every right purpose;
direct this hour of worship to the magnifying of Thy name,
and to the enduring good of us Thy children and servants;
through Jesus Christ our Lord. Amen.

D. PRAYERS OF GENERAL CONFESSION

In the prayer of confession the worshipper asks divine forgiveness for his sins; this is a necessary prelude to the fit
worship of God. This prayer should be preceded by some
such sentence as this: "Let us now humbly and earnestly
confess our sins unto Almighty God, using the prayer found
_____." If the members of the congregation do not have a
service book or worship folder from which they can read the
prayer, you may request that they repeat the prayer after
you, a phrase at a time. Following this prayer, you should
lead the worshippers in repeating in unison the Lord's Prayer.

(1 Almighty and most merciful Father, we have erred,
and strayed from Thy ways like lost sheep. We have followed too much the devices and desires of our own hearts.
We have offended against Thy holy laws. We have left undone those things which we ought to have done; and we have
done those things which we ought not to have done; and there
is no health in us. But Thou, O Lord, have mercy upon us,
miserable offenders. Spare Thou those, O God, who confess
their faults. Restore Thou those who are penitent; according
to Thy promises declared unto mankind in Christ Jesus our
Lord. And grant, O most merciful Father, for His sake,
that we may hereafter live a godly, righteous, and sober life,
to the glory of thy Holy Name. Amen.

(2) Have mercy upon us, O Lord, according to Thy loving kindness; according to the multitude of Thy tender mercies blot out our transgressions. Wash us thoroughly from
our iniquities and cleanse us from our sins. For we acknowledge our transgressions and our sin is ever before us.
Create in us clean hearts, O God and renew a right spirit
within us; through Jesus Christ our Lord. Amen.

(3) Almighty and eternal God, who searchest the hearts
of men, we acknowledge and confess that we have sinned
against Thee in thought word, and deed; that we have not
loved Thee with all our heart and soul, with all our mind and
strength; and that we have not loved our neighbor as our -
selves. Forgive us our transgressions, and help us to a-
mend our ways, and of Thine eternal goodness direct what we
shall be, so that we may henceforth walk in the way of Thy
commandments, and do those things which are worthy in Thy
sight; through Jesus Christ our Lord. Amen.

(4) Almighty God, unto whom all hearts are open, all desires known, and from whom no secrets are hid; cleanse the
thoughts of our hearts by the inspiration of thy Holy Spirit,
that we may perfectly love Thee, and worthily magnify Thy
Holy Name, through Jesus Christ our Lord. Amen

E. <u>A PRAYER FOR PARDON</u>

Following the general prayer of confession, or a period of
silent confession, the lay leader may offer a short prayer
for pardon before leading the congregation in the Lord's
Prayer.

(1) May the almighty and merciful Lord grant us remission of all our sins, true repentance, amendment of life,
and the grace and consolation of his Holy Spirit. Amen.

(2) O Lord, we beseech thee, mercifully hear our prayers, and spare all those who confess their sins unto Thee,
that they whose consciences by sin are accused, by Thy
merciful pardon may be absolved; through Christ our Lord.
Amen.

(3) May almighty God, who caused light to shine out of
darkness, shine in our hearts, cleansing us from all our
sins, and restoring us to the light of the knowledge of His
glory in the face of Jesus Christ our Lord. Amen.

(4) O Lord, we beseech Thee, forgive Thy people their of-
tenses, that through Thy bountiful goodness we may be delivered
from the bends of those sins which by our frailty we have
committed. Grant this, O Heavenly Father, for Jesus Christ's
sake, our blessed Lord and Saviour. Amen.

F. THE LORD'S PRAYER

Following the Prayer of General Confession, or the Prayer of
Pardon, the Lord's Prayer should be repeated by the congregation in unison. This is the most ancient prayer of the
Christian church, and taught by Jesus Christ Himself. It may
he introduced with these words. "Let us now repeat together
the prayer taught us by our Lord. Our Father who art in
heaven

> Our Father who art in heaven, hallowed be Thy name. Thy
> Kingdom come. Thy will be done. on earth as it is in
> heaven. Give us this day our daily bread, and forgive us
> our trespasses as we forgive those who trespass against
> us. And lead us not into temptation, but deliver us from
> evil. For Thine is the Kingdom, and the Power, and the
> Glory forever. Amen,

Upon concluding the Lord's Prayer, it is recommended and
altogether fitting that you remind the worshipers of God's
promise to forgive the sins of those who humbly repent and
turn from their sins. A scriptural assurance of pardon, such
as the two which follow, may be repeated.

> "If we confess our sins. He is faithful and just to forgive
> us our sins and to cleanse us from all unrighteousness.

> "For God so loved the world, that He gave His only begotten
> son: that whosoever believeth in Him should not perish bet
> have everlasting life.

NOTE: A lay leader is not permitted to pronounce absolution.

G. SPECIAL MUSIC

Although it is unlikely that special music will be available to
you in the field, nevertheless it may be included at this point
in the service per chance a choir, quartet, or soloist is ob-
tainable. The choir's anthem or the soloist's number should
be a selection which expresses worship and praise to God.
Remember, a choir and quartet does not have to be polished
to fulfill a useful function in the service. If it gives some
men an opportunity for service in the worship of God and brings
to others a message from God, it belongs in the order of worship.

H. THE RESPONSIVE READING

The Responsive Reading is another means whereby the congregation takes an active role in worshipping God: God's Word is read, spiritually ingested, and meditated upon. The Scripture portions shown below are suggested for this purpose. As the leader, begin by reading the first sentence. The congregation is to then read the second sentence, and alternate with you for the remainder of the passage.

In order to enable the congregation to participate in this part of the service, you may do one of the following: (1) make copies (one for every two or three men) of the scripture portion (mimeographed, typed, or hand written), or (2) hand out New Testaments, Service Books, copies of "Song and Service Book", or worship folders which either include a Responsive Reading or a passage of scripture that can be so read.

If you choose your own Responsive Reading from the New Testament, for instance, you are reminded that the book of Psalms is a splendid and particularly appropriate source. Choose a passage which will speak to a man's need, strengthening him if he be weak, cheering him if he be despondent, and giving him hope if he be downhearted.

(1) Come With Thanksgiving

Lay Leader:

O go your way into His gates with thanksgiving and into His courts with praise: be thankful unto Him, and speak ye good of His Name. For the Lord is gracious, His mercy is everlasting: and His truth endureth from generation to generation

Lay Leader and PEOPLE:

O come let us sing unto the Lord:
LET US MAKE A JOYFUL NOISE TO THE ROCK OF OUR
SALVATION.

Let us come before His presence with thanksgiving:
AND MAKE A JOYFUL NOISE UNTO HIM WITH PSALMS.

For the Lord is a great God:
AND A GREAT KING ABOVE ALL GODS.

In His hand are the deep places of the earth:
  THE STRENGTH OF THE HILLS IS HIS ALSO.

The sea is His, and He made it:
  AND HIS HANDS FORMED THE DRY LAND.

O come, let us worship and bow down:
  LET US KNEEL BEFORE THE LORD OUR MAKER.

For He is our God and we are the people of His pasture:
  AND THE SHEEP OF HIS HAND.
Today if ye will hear His voice:
  HARDEN NOT YOUR HEART.

Lay Leader:

Behold, the tabernacle of God is with men, and He shall dwell
with them, and they shall be His people, and God Himself
shall be with them and be their God: And He shall wipe away
every tear from their eyes; and death shall be no more; and
neither shall there be mourning, nor crying, nor pain any
more: the first things are passed away.

  (2) Seek Ye The Lord

Lay Leader   Isaiah 55

Seek ye the Lord while He may be found, call ye upon Him
while He is near: Let the wicked forsake his way, and the un-
righteous man his thoughts: and let him return unto the Lord,
and He will have mercy upon him; and to our God, for He
will abundantly pardon.

Lay Leader and PEOPLE: Psalm 27

Hear, O Lord, when I cry with my voice:
  HAVE MERCY ALSO UPON ME, AND ANSWER ME.

When Thou saidst, Seek ye my face:
  MY HEART SAID UNTO THEE, THY FACE, LORD, WILL I
  SEEK

Hide not Thy face far from me:
  PUT NOT THY SERVANT AWAY IN ANGER.

Thou hast been my help:
  LEAVE ME NOT, NEITHER FORSAKE ME, O God OF MY
  SALVATION.

When my father and my mother forsake me:
    THEN THE LORD WILL TAKE ME UP.

Teach me Thy way, O Lord:
    AND LEAD ME IN A PLAIN PATH, BECAUSE OF MINE
    ENEMIES.

Deliver me not over unto the will of mine enemies:
    FOR FALSE WITNESSES ARE RISEN UP AGAINST ME, AND
    SUCH AS BREATHE OUT CRUELTY.

I had fainted unless I had believed to see the goodness of the
Lord in the land of the living.
    WAIT ON THE LORD, BE OF GOOD COURAGE, AND HE
    SHALL STRENGTHEN THINE HEART: WAIT, I SAY, ON
    THE LORD.

Lay Leader   Luke 19

Jesus saith ... The Son of Man is come to seek and to save
that which was lost.

Lay Leader   John 3

For God sent not his Son into the world to condemn the world;
but that the world through Him might be saved.

   (3) The Fear Of The Lord

Lay Leader   Ecclesiastes 12

Fear God and keep His commandments; for this Is the whole
duty of man. For God shall bring every work Into judgment,
with every secret thing, whether it be good, or whether it be
evil.

Lay Leader and PEOPLE: Psalm 24

Come, ye children, hearken unto me:
    I WILL TEACH YOU THE FEAR OF THE LORD.

What man is he that desireth life:
    AND LOVETH MANY DAYS, THAT HE MAY SEE GOOD?

Keep thy tongue from evil:
    AND THY LIPS FROM SPEAKING GUILE.

Depart from evil, and do good:
  SEEK PEACE, AND PURSUE IT.

The eyes of the Lord are upon the righteous:
  AND HIS EARS ARE OPEN UNTO THEIR CRY.

The face of the Lord is against them that do evil:
  TO CUT OFF THE REMEMBRANCE OF THEM FROM THE
  EARTH.

The Lord is nigh unto them that are of a broken heart:
  AND SAVETH SUCH AS BE OF A CONTRITE SPIRIT.

Many are the afflictions of the righteous:
  BUT THE LORD DELIVERETH HIM OUT OF THEM ALL.

The Lord redeemeth the soul of His servants:
  AND NONE OF THEM THAT TRUST IN HIM SHALL BE
  DESOLATE.

<u>Lay Leader</u>:   Proverbs 9

The fear of the Lord is the beginning of wisdom; and the
knowledge of the Holy is understanding. For by wisdom thy
days shall be multiplied, and the years of thy life increased.

    (4) <u>Trust In The Lord</u>

<u>Lay Leader</u>:   Job 5

Behold, happy is the man whom God correcteth: Therefore despise not thou the chastening of the Almighty. For He maketh
sore. and He bindeth up; He woundeth and His hands make
whole. He shall deliver thee in six troubles; ye, in seven
there shall no evil touch thee.

<u>Lay Leader and PEOPLE</u>:   Psalm 63

O God, Thou art my God:
  EARLY WILL I SEEK THEE,

My soul thirsteth for Thee:
  MY FLESH LONGETH FOR THEE IN A DRY AND THIRSTY
  I AND, WHERE NO WATER IS;

To see Thy power and Thy glory:
  SO I HAVE SEEN THEE IN THE SANCTUARY.

Because Thy loving kindness is better than life:
    MY LIPS SHALL PRAISE THEE.

Thus will I bless Thee while I live:
    I WILL LIFT UP MY HANDS IN THY NAME.

My soul shall be satisfied as with marrow and fatness;
    AND MY MOUTH SHALL PRAISE THEE WITH JOYFUL LIPS

When I remember Thee upon my bed:
    AND MEDITATE ON THEE IN THE NIGHT WATCHES.

Because Thou hast been my help:
    THEREFORE IN THE SHADOW OF THY WINGS WILL I RE-
    JOICE.

My soul followeth hard after Thee:
    THY RIGHT HAND UPHOLDETH ME,

<u>Lay leader</u>:   Psalm 36

Trust in the Lord, and do good; delight thyself also in the
lord; and He shall give thee the desires of thine heart.
Commit thy way unto the Lord; trust also in Him; and He shall
bring it to pass.

I. <u>THE CREED OR AFFIRMATION OF FAITH</u>

An affirmation of faith has traditionally been a part of Christian worship. Such an affirmation, repeated in unison, re-
minds the worshippers of the primary beliefs of the Christian
faith to which they profess allegiance, and gives them a feel-
ing of belonging to the entire church of Christ. Either one of
the following affirmations may be used. It may be made a-
vailable to the congregation as indicated in (H) above.

The lay leader may like to preface the reciting of the Creed
by saying:

"Where the Spirit of the Lord is, there is the one true
Church, apostolic and universal, whose Holy Faith let us now
reverently and sincerely declare."

(1) The Apostle's Creed

I believe in God the Father Almighty, Maker of Heaven and
earth: and in Jesus Christ his only Son, our Lord; who was
conceived by the Holy Ghost; born of the Virgin Mary, suffered

under Pontius Pilate, was crucified, dead and buried; He
descended into hell; the third day He rose again from the dead;
He ascended into heaven and sitteth on the right hand of God
the Father Almighty; from thence He shall come to judge the
quick and the dead. I believe in the Holy Ghost: the holy
catholic church: the communion of saints the forgiveness of
sins; the resurrection of the body and the life everlasting.
Amen.

(2)   The Declaration of Faith

I believe in God our Father, infinite in wisdom, goodness,
and love, and in his Son, our Saviour, the Lord Jesus Christ,
Who for us men and our salvation lived and died and liveth
evermore, exalted at the right hand of the Father, whose
kingdom shall have no end. And I believe in the Holy Spirit
of God, the Lord and Giver of Life, proceeding from the
Father and the Son, and with the Father and the Son exalted
and glorified; taking of the things of Christ, revealing hem
to us; comforting, renewing, inspiring our spirit. I believe in
the persistence of personality and immortality of the soul, and
I look for the victory of righteousness over evil, life over
death, and for the life of the world to come. Amen.

J.   THE SCRIPTURE LESSON

The Scripture Lesson is a portion of the Bible which you read
to the congregation. In prayer, we speak to God; through the
reading of Scripture, God speaks to us. The Bible passage
should be read reverently, distinctly and in a voice enabling
all to clearly hear and understand. Further it should be re-
lated to the message (M), if there is one. Possibly it will
be a springboard for the remarks which are made, providing
illustrative or background material for them. If there is no
message, then a scripture lesson should be chosen which itself is a message: God's word to His Children in which they
are exhorted and instructed in godliness and Christian living.
By all means choose carefully a passage which will find ap-
plication and meaning in the minds and hearts of the hearers:
the genealogy of the 1st chapter of St. Matthew, for instance,
would not be advise&

Any one of the Scripture Lessons which follows, or an appro-
priately chosen portion from your New Testament or Service
Book, may be read at this point in the service.

(1)   St. John 1:1-14

1.   In the beginning was the Word, and the Word was with
     God, and the Word was God.

2. The same was in the beginning with God.
3. All things were made by him; and without him was not any thing made that was made.
4. In him was life; and the life was the light of men.
5. And the light shineth in darkness; and the darkness comprehended it not.
6. There was a man sent from God, whose name was John.
7. The same came for a witness, to bear witness of the light, that all men through him might believe.
8. He was not that Light, but was sent to bear witness of that Light.
9. That was the true light, which lighteth every man that cometh into the world.
10. He was in the world, and the world was made by him, and the world knew him not.
11. He came unto his own, and his own received him not.
12. But as many as received him, to them gave he power to become the sons of God, even to them that believe on his name:
13. Which were born, not of blood, nor of the will of the flesh, nor of the will of man, but of God.
14. And the Word was made flesh, and dwelt among us, (and we beheld his glory, the glory as of the only begotten of the Father,) full of grace and truth.

(2) St. John 14:1-21

1. Let not your heart be troubled: ye believe in God. Believe also in me.
2. In my Father's house are many mansions: if it were not so, I would have told you. I go to prepare a place for you.
3 And if I go and prepare a place for you, I will come again, and receive you unto myself: that where I am, there ye may be also.
4. And whither I go ye know, and the way ye know.
5. Thomas saith unto him, Lord, we know not whither thou goest: and how can we know the way?
6. Jesus saith unto him, I am the way, the truth. and the life: no man cometh unto the Father, but by me.
7. If ye had known me. ye should have known my Father also; and from henceforth ye know him, and have seen him,
8. Philip saith unto him, Lord, show us the Father, and it sufficeth us.
9. Jesus saith unto him. Have I been so long time with you, and yet hast thou not known me, Philip? He that hath seen me hath seen the Father: and how sayest thou then, Show us the Father?

10. Believest thou not that I am in the Father, and the Father in me? the words that I speak unto you I speak not of myself: but the Father that dwelleth in me, he doeth the works.

11. Believe me that I am in the Father, and the Father in me: or else believe me for the very works' sake.

12. Verily, verily, I say unto you, He that believeth in me, the works that I do shall he do also; and greater works than these shall he do; because I go unto my Father.

13. And whatsoever ye shall ask in my name, that will I do, that the Father may he glorified in the Son.

14. If ye shall ask any thing in my name, I will do it.

15. If ye love me, keep my commandments.

16. And I will pray the Father, and he shall give you another Comforter, that he may abide with you forever;

17. Even the Spirit of truth; whom the world cannot receive, because it seeth him not, neither knoweth him; but ye know him; for he dwelleth with you, and shall be in you.

18. I will not leave you comfortless: I will come to you.

19. Yet a little while, and the world seeth me no more; but ye see me: because I live, ye shall live also.

20. At that day ye shall know that I am in my Father, and ye in me, and I in you.

21. He that hath my commandments, and keepeth them, he it is that loveth me: and he that loveth me shall be loved of my Father, and I will love him, and will manifest myself to him.

(3)   I Corinthians 13:1-13

1. Though I speak with the tongues of men and of angels, and have not charity, I am become as sounding brass, or a tinkling cymbal.

2. And though I have the gift of prophecy, and understand all mysteries, and all knowledge; and though I have all faith, so that I could remove mountains, and have not charity, I am nothing.

3. And though I bestow all my goods to feed the poor, and though I give my body to be burned, and have not charity, it profiteth me nothing

4. Charity suffereth long, and is kind; charity envieth not; charity vaunteth not itself, is not puffed up,

5. Doth not behave itself unseemly, seeketh not her own, is not easily provoked, thinketh no evil;

6. Rejoiceth not in iniquity, but rejoiceth in the truth;

7. Beareth all things, believeth all things, hopeth all things, endureth all things.

8. Charity never faileth; but whether there be prophecies they shall fail; whether there be tongues, they shall cease; whether there be knowledge, it shall vanish away.

9. For we know in part, and we prophesy in part,
10. But when that which is perfect is come, then that which is in part shall be done away.
11. When I was a child, I spake as a child, I understood as a child, I thought as a child: but when I became a man, I put away childish things.
12. For now we see through a glass, darkly; but then face to face; now I know in part; but then shall I know even as also I am known
13. And now abideth faith, hope, charity, these three: but the greatest of these is charity.

(4)   James 1:12-27

12. Blessed is the man that endureth temptation: for when he is tried, he shall receive the crown of life, which the Lord hath promised to them that love him.
13. Let no man say when he is tempted. I am tempted of God: for God cannot be tempted with evil, neither tempteth he any man:
14. But every man is tempted, when he is drawn away of his own lust, and enticed.
15. Then when lust hath conceived, it bringeth forth sin; and sin, when it is finished, bringeth forth death.
16. Do not err, my beloved brethren.
17. Every good gift and every perfect gift is from above, and cometh down from the Father of lights, with whom is no variableness, neither shadow of turning.
18. of his own will begat he us with the word of truth, that we should be a kind of first fruits of his creatures.
19. Wherefore, my beloved brethren, let every man be swift to hear, slow to speak, slow to wrath:
20, For the wrath of man worketh not the righteousness of God.
21. Wherefore lay apart all filthiness and superfluity of naughtiness, and receive with meekness the engrafted word, which is able to save your souls.
22. But be ye doers of the word, and not hearers only, deceiving your own selves.
23. For if any be a hearer of the word, and not a doer, he is like unto a man beholding his natural face in a glass:
24. For he beholdeth himself, and goeth his way, and straightway forgetteth what manner of man he was.
25. But whoso looketh into the perfect law of liberty, and continueth therein, he being not a forgetful hearer, but a doer of the work, this man shall be blessed in his deed.
26. If any man among you seem to be religious, and bridleth not his tongue, but deceiveth his own heart, this man's religion is vain.

27. Pure religion and undefiled before God and the Father is this, To visit the fatherless and widows in their affliction, and to keep himself unspotted from the world.

(5) Additional Scripture Readings

A Soldier's Life: Luke 3:14; Matt. 8:5-13: Acts 10; II Cor. 10:3-5; Eph. 6:10-18; II Tim. 2:3,4; Rev. 12:7-11; Rev. 19: 11-21

On the Sea: Luke 5:3; Mark 4:35-41; Matt. 14:13-23; John 21 :1-24; Acts 27,

Sin and Temptation: Psalms 6, 31, 143; Matt. 4:1-11; Mark 9:43-487 Luke 21:34-36; John 8:34-36; Rom. 2:1-6; I Cor. 6: 15-20; Gal. 6:1-10; James 1:2-8;12-27; James 4; I John 1:6-10.

Repentance and Forgiveness: Psalms 25, 40, 77; Matt. 9, 12, 13; Matt. 11:28-30; Matt. 18:21-35; Luke 7:36-50; Luke 15; Luke 17:3, 4; Luke 19:1-10; John 6:35-37; John 8, 12; Acts 4:12; 11 Cor. 5:20,21; Eph. 1:7: I Tim. 1:15; Hebrews 7:24-27; Hebrews 10:11-25; I John 1:7; Rev. 2:1-5; Rev. 3:14 -21.

Christian Life: Matt. 8:31-38; Luke 14:25-35; Rom. 6:3-14; Rom. 12:9-21; I Cor. 13; Gal. 5:14-26; Eph. 4:1-6; Phil. 3:7 -14; Hebrews 12:11-17; James 3; I Pet. 5:6-11; I John 2:12-17.

Prayer: Psalms 40, 42, 55; Matt. 6:5-15; Luke 11:1-13; John 4:46-54; John 14:13, 14; John 16:23-27: James 5:13-18.

Affliction: Psalms 22, 74, 102; John 16; II Tim. 3:12-17; Hebrews 2:9, 10, 14-18

Assurance: Psalms 3, 16, 27; Rom. 8:31-39; Eph. 3:14-21; Hebrews 11.

Protection: Psalms 23, 34, 91; Luke 1, 6, 7; Hebrews 13: 5, 6.

Thanksgiving: Psalms 9, 34, 103; Luke 1:68-75; Luke 17: 11-19

The Life Beyond: Luke 2:29-32; Luke 16:19-31; 1 Cor. 15: 12-26, 50-58; 11 Cor. 5, 1-10; II Tim. 1:10; Hebrews 13:14; Rev. 19:11-21; Rev. 21:1; Rev. 22:5,

PRAYERS OF THANKSGIVING AND SUPPLICATION

Depending upon your own church background and convictions, you may prefer to give an extemporaneous prayer. If you do however, beware that your prayer is not casual, repititious, disjointed, or devoid of vital religious meaning. Also make certain that it has been prepared beforehand at least in your own heart and mind. And that it contains both Thanksgiving to God for his blessing and benefits, and Intercession for the needs of others. It Is difficult to maintain a true attitude of prayer for long. Jesus' prayers were short. A prayer of over one minute and a half is not recommended. For the average lay leader, it Is recommended that a prepared prayer be used. You may write it yourself, keeping in mind the points mentioned above. Or you may use one of the prayers which follows.

(1) For The Marine Corps: Saint Francis' Prayer

Lord make me a channel of Thy peace. That where there is hatred- - I may bring love. That where there is wrong--I may bring the spirit of forgiveness. That where there is discord--I may bring harmony. That where there is error- - I may bring truth. That where there is doubt- -I may bring faith. That where there is despair--I may bring hope.   That where there are shadows - -I may bring light. That where there is sadness--I may bring Joy. Lord, grant that I may seek rather to comfort--than to be comforted: to understand than to be understood: To love- -than to be loved: For it is by giving- -that one receives: It is by self-forgetting that one finds: It is by dying- -that one awakens to eternal life. Amen.

-Saint Francis of Assisi

(2) For Safe Deliverance

Almighty and everlasting God, in whom we live and move and have our being; We, Thy needy creatures, render Thee our humble praises, for Thy preservation of us from the beginning of our lives to this day, and especially for having delivered us from the dangers of the past night. For these Thy mercies, we bless and magnify Thy glorious Name; humbly beseeching Thee to accept this our morning sacrifice of praise and thanksgiving; for His sake who lay down In the grave, and rose again for us, thy Son our Saviour Jesus Christ, Amen.

-Book of Common Prayer

(3) For Grace To Love and Serve God

Almighty God, Who alone gavest us the breath of life, and
Who by Thy Spirit dost keep alive in us all holy desires: We
beseech Thee, for Thy compassion's sake, to sanctify all our
thoughts and endeavors, so that we may neither begin an ac-
tion without a pure intention nor continue it without Thy blessing, hut walking with Thee this day we may both purpose and
accomplish that which is wholly pleasing to Thee; through
Jesus Christ, thy Son, our Lord. Amen.

(4) In Time Of Temptation

Lord and Master, Jesus Christ. who thyself wast tempted
as we are, yet without sin, give me grace to meet this
temptation which now assails me and which I would overcome.
Enable me to check all evil thoughts and passions, all entice-
ments to self-indulgence or dishonest gain, and to find. like
thee, my highest satisfactions in the doing of my Heavenly
Father's will. Amen.

(5) For Loved Ones

O Thou who hast ordered this wondrous world, who knowest
all things in earth and heaven; so fill our hearts with trust in
thee, that by night and by day, at all times and in all seasons
we may without fear commit those who are dear to us to Thy
never-failing love for this life and the life to come. Through
Jesus Christ our Lord, Amen.

For our absent loved ones we implore Thy loving kindness.
Keep them in life, keep them in growing honour; and for us,
grant that we may remain worthy of their love. For Christ's
sake, let not our beloved blush for us, nor we for them.
Grant us but that, and grant us courage to endure lesser ills
unshaken, and to accept death, loss, and disappointment as it
were straws upon the tide of life, Amen.

O God, who art present to Thy faithful people in every
place, mercifully hear our prayers for those we love who are
now parted from us. Watch over them, we beseech Thee, and
protect them in all anxiety, danger and temptation; and teach
us and them to feel and know that Thou art always near and
that we are one in Thee forever; through Jesus Christ our
Lord. Amen.

L.　HYMNS OF PREPARATION

(1) What a Friend We Have in Jesus

What a friend we have in Jesus,
All our sins and griefs to hear!
What a privilege to carry,
Everything to God in Prayer!
O what peace we often forfeit,
o what a needless pain we hear,
All because we do not carry
Everything to God in prayer.

Have we trials and temptations?
Is there trouble anywhere?
We should never be discouraged:
Take it to the Lord in prayer.
Can we find a friend so faithful,
who will all our sorrows share?
Jesus knows our every weakness;
Take It to the Lord in prayer!

Are we weak and heavy laden,
Cumbered with a load of care?
Precious Saviour, still our Refuge;
Take it to the Lord in prayer!
Do thy friends despise, forsake thee?
Take it to the Lord in prayer!
In His arms He'll take and shield thee,
Thou wilt find a solace there. A-men.

(2) The Old Rugged Cross

On a hill far away stood an old rugged cross,
The emblem of suffering and shame;
And I love that old cross where the dearest and hest
For a world of lost sinners was slain.

Chorus:

So I'll cherish the old rugged cross
Till my trophies at last I lay down;
I will cling to the old rugged cross,
And exchange it some day for a crown.

Oh, that old rugged cross, so despised by the world,
Has a wondrous attraction for me;
For the dear Lamb of God left His glory above
To hear it to dark Calvary.

Chorus:

In the old rugged cross, stained with blood so divine,
A wondrous beauty I see;
For 'twas on that old cross Jesus suffered and died
To pardon and sanctify me.

Chorus:

To the old rugged cross I will ever be true,
Its shame and reproach gladly bear;
Then He'll call me some day to my home far away,
Where His glory forever I'll share.

Chorus:

(3) Dear Lord and Father of Mankind

Dear Lord and Father of mankind,
Forgive our foolish ways;
Reclothe us in our rightful mind,
In purer lives Thy service find,
In deeper reverence, praise.

In simple trust like theirs who heard,
Beside the Syrian sea,
The gracious calling of the Lord,
Let us, like them, without a word
Rise up and follow Thee.

O Sabbath rest by Galilee,
O calm of hills above,
Where Jesus knelt to share with Thee
The silence of eternity,
Interpreted by love!

Drop Thy still dews of quietness,
Till all our strivings cease;
Take from our souls the strain and stress,
And let our ordered lives confess
The beauty of Thy peace.

Breathe through the heats of our desire
Thy coolness and Thy balm;
Let sense be dumb, let flesh retire;
Speak through the earth-quake, wind and fire,
O still, small voice of calm!

A-men.

(4) The Church's One Foundation
The Church1s one Foundation
Is Jesus Christ her Lord;
She is His new creation
By water and the word:
From heaven He came and sought her
To he His holy Bride
With His own blood He bought her,
And for her life He die&

Elect from every nation,
Yet one o'er all the earth,
Her charter of salvation
One Lord, one faith, one birth;
One holy name she blesses,
Partakes one holy food,
And to one hope she presses,
With every grace endued.

Mid toil and tribulation,
And tumult of her war,
She waits the consummation
Of peace for ever more;
Till with the vision glorious,
Her longing eyes are blest,
And the great Church victorious
Shall be the Church at rest.

Yet she on earth hath union
With God the Three in One,
And mystic sweet communion
With those whose rest is won:
O happy ones and holy!
Lord, give us grace that we,
Like them, the meek and lowly,
On high may dwell with Thee.   A-men.

M.   THE MESSAGE

First see your chaplain for instructions in this regard. Regulations do not permit lay leaders to engage in formal preach-
lag largely because we must respect the rights of conscience
of many people of many churches who believe that this right
is conferred only on those who are ordained clergymen.

There are many messages prepared by our church leaders
for use by lay leaders which are available to you through your
chaplain.

N.   THE HYMN OF DEDICATION

(1) When I Survey The Wondrous Cross

When I survey the wondrous cross
On which the Prince of Glory died,
My richest gain I count but loss,
And pour contempt on all my pride.

Forbid it, Lord, that I should boast,
Save in the death of Christ my God;
All the vain things that charm me most,
I sacrifice them to His blood.

See from His head, His hands, His feet,
Sorrow, and love flow mingled down:
Did e'er such love and sorrow meet,
Or thorns compose so rich a crown?

Were the whole realm of nature mine,
That were a present far too small;
Love so amazing, so divine
Demands my soul, my life, my all.

(2) Rise Up, O Men of God'

Rise up, O men of God!
Have done with lesser things;
Give heart and soul and mind and strength
To serve the King of Kings.

Rise up, O men of God!
His Kingdom tarries long;
Bring in the day of brotherhood
And end the night of wrong

Rise up, O men of God!
The Church for you doth wait,
Her strength unequal to her task;
Rise up, and make her great!

Lift high the cross of Christ!
Tread where His feet have trod;
As brothers of the Son of Man,
Rise up, O men of God.

                    A-men.

(3) Jesus Keep Me Near The Cross

Jesus, keep me near the cross;
There a precious fountain
Free to all, a healing stream,
Flows from Calvary's mountain.
<u>Refrain</u>:

In the cross, in the cross
Be my glory ever,
Till my raptured soul shall find
Rest beyond the river.

Near the cross, a trembling soul
Love and mercy found me;
There the bright and morning Star
Sheds its beams around me.

Near the cross!   O Lamb of God,
Bring its scenes before me;
Help me walk from day to day,
With its shadow o'er me.

Near the cross I'll watch and wait;
Hoping, trusting ever,
Till I reach the golden strand,
Just beyond the river.

(4) My Jesus I Love Thee

My Jesus, I love Thee, I know Thou art mine,
For Thee all the follies of sin I resign;
My gracious Redeemer, my Saviour art Thou;
If ever I loved Thee, my Jesus 'tis now.

I love Thee because Thou hast first loved me,
And purchased my pardon on Calvary's tree;
I love Thee for wearing the thorns on Thy brow;
If ever I loved Thee, my Jesus 'tis now.

I will love Thee in life, I will love Thee in death,
And praise Thee as long as Thou lendest me breath;
And say when the death dew lies cold on my brow;
If ever I loved Thee, my Jesus 'tis now.

In mansions of glory and endless delight,
I'll ever adore Thee in heaven so bright:
I'll sing with the glittering crown on my brow,
If ever I loved Thee, my Jesus 'tis now. A-men.

(5) Lead On, O King Eternal

Lead on, O King Eternal,
The day of march has come;
Henceforth in field of conquest
Thy tents shall be our home;
Through days of preparation
Thy grace has made us strong,
And now, O King Eternal,
We lift our battle song.

Lead on, O King Eternal,
Till sin's fierce war shall cease,
And Holiness shall whisper
The sweet Amen of peace;
For not with swords' loud clashing,
Nor roll of stirring drums,
With deeds of love and mercy,
The heavenly Kingdom comes.

Lead on, O King Eternal:
We follow, not with fears;
For gladness breaks like morning
Wher'er Thy face appears;
Thy cross is lifted o'er us;
We journey in its light;
The crown awaits the conquest;
Lead on, O God of might. A-men.

(6) Eternal Father, Strong To Save

Eternal Father, strong to save,
Whose arm hath bound the restless wave,
Who bidd'st the mighty ocean deep,
Its own appointed limits keep;
O hear us when we cry to Thee
For those in peril on the sea.

O Saviour whose almighty word
The winds and waves submissive heard,
Who walked'st on the foaming deep,
And calm amidst its rage didst sleep;
O hear us when we cry to Thee
For those in peril on the sea.

Eternal Father, grant, we pray,
To all Marines, both night and day,
The courage, honor, strength and skill
Their land to serve, Thy law fulfill;
Be Thou the Shield forevermore
From ev'ry peril to the Corps.

O Trinity of love and power,
Our brethren shield in danger's hour;
From rock and tempest, fire and foe,
Protect them whereso e'er they go,
Thus ever let there rise to Thee
Glad praise from land and sea. A-men.

O.   THE CLOSING PRAYER

The service should be concluded with one of the following:

(1) O most gracious and merciful God, grant that what hath
been dose be our devotion and service may be confirmed by
Thy benediction; through our Lord Jesus Christ. Amen.

(2) Dismiss us now, O Lord, with Thy blessing, and ac-
company us ever with Thy grace, that we may henceforth live
in peace, love and holiness through Jesus Christ our Lord.
Amen.

(3) O Lord, Father Almighty, bless and sanctify this sacrifice of praise which has been offered unto Thee, to the honor
and glory of Thy name; through Jesus Christ our Lord. Amen.

(4) Grant, O Lord, that what hath been said with our lips
we may believe in our hearts, and that what we believe in our
hearts we may practice in our lives; through Jesus Christ our
Lord. Amen.

SECTION VIII

THE CATHOLIC LAY LEADER

WORSHIP SERVICE

As a Catholic Lay Leader you are not permitted to offer Mass,
which is the official Catholic act of worship. Nor can you
administer the Sacraments. You can however, lead a non-
liturgical, devotional service which will be pleasing to God
and spiritually beneficial to your fellow Marines.

The traditional Catholic Lay Leader service is the Rosary
Service. As the name implies, the basis of the service is

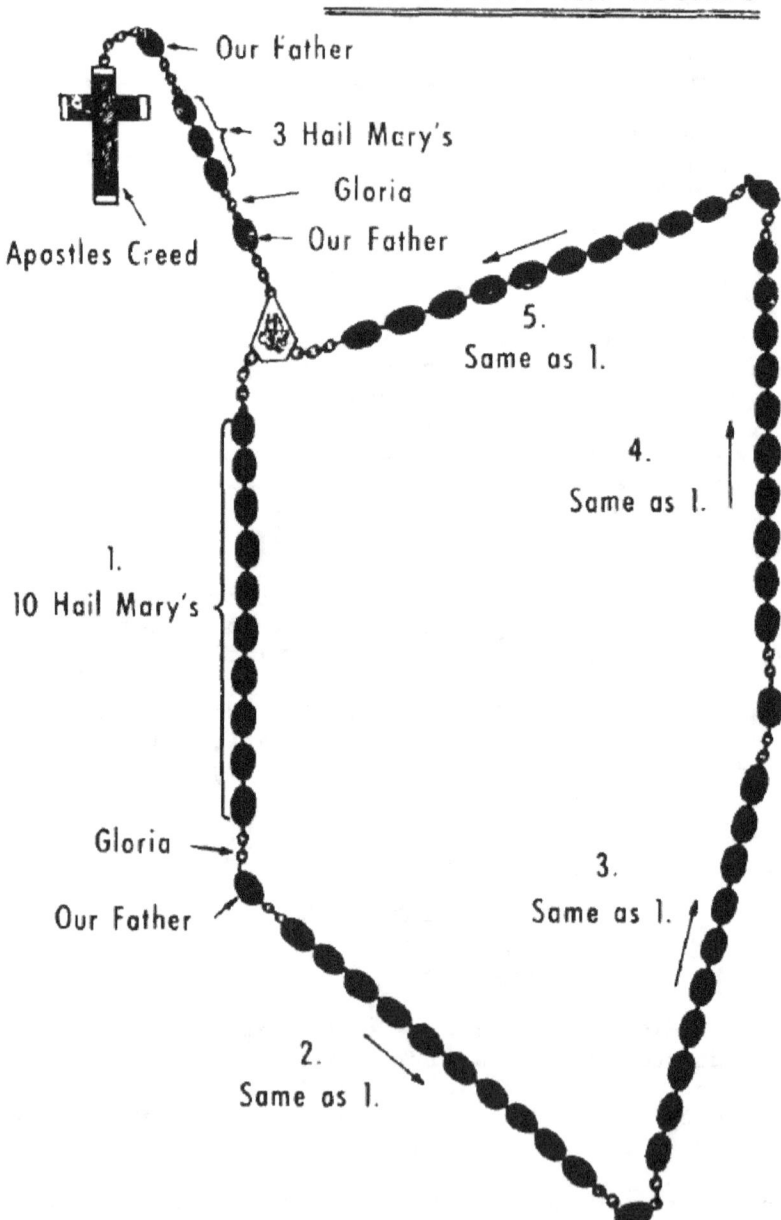

Our Father

3 Hail Mary's

Gloria

Our Father

Apostles Creed

5.
Same as 1.

4.
Same as 1.

1.
10 Hail Mary's

Gloria

Our Father

3.
Same as 1.

2.
Same as 1.

the recitation of the Rosary. The service can be led by the
lay leader, or another qualified Marine who you may appoint.
The entire Rosary is made up of fifteen sections, or decades.
However, only five decades are usually included in the service; this will be the service which you conduct. On the op-
posite page the manner of saying the Rosary is illustrated.
Following are the prayers which are used:

The * indicates where the congregation begins its response.

1. Prayers of the Rosary

APOSTLES CREED: I believe in God, the Father Almighty,
Creator of heaven and earth; and in Jesus Christ, his only
Son, Our Lord; who was conceived by the Holy Ghost; horn of
the Virgin Mary, suffered under Pontius Pilate, was crucified,
died and was buried. He descended into hell; the third day
He arose again from the dead; He ascended into heaven, sitteth at the right hand of God, the Father Almighty; from thence
He shall come to judge the living and the dead. * I believe in
the Holy Ghost, the Holy Catholic Church, the communion of
saints, the forgiveness of sins, the resurrection of the body,
and life everlasting. Amen.

OUR FATHER: Our Father who art in heaven, hallowed be
Thy name; Thy kingdom come; Thy will be done on earth as it
is In heaven. * Give us this day our daily bread; and forgive
us our trespasses as we forgive those who trespass against
us; and lead us not into temptation, but deliver us from evil.
Amen.

HAIL MARY: Hail Mary, full of grace! The Lord is with
thee; blessed are thou among women, and blessed is the fruit
of thy womb, Jesus. * Holy Mary, Mother of God. Pray for
us sinners, now, and at the hour of our death. Amen.

GLORIA: Glory be to the Father, and to the Son, and to
the Holy Ghost. * As it was in the beginning, is now, and
ever shall be world without end. Amen.

2. The Mysteries Of The Rosary

The purpose of this ancient Rosary devotion is two-fold: to
honor the Mother of God, and to teach the life of Christ. To
fulfill the second purpose, we should meditate on, or think
over, a different scene from Christ's life during each decade.
The lay leader names the mystery and should read a short

explanation of it.   (Father Peyton's Rosary Prayer Book is a valuable help in doing this.)

A.   JOYFUL MYSTERIES (Monday and Thursday)

(1)   The Angel Gabriel announces to Mary that she is to be the Mother of God (Luke 1:26-38)
(2)   Mary visits her cousin Elizabeth.   (Luke 1:39-56)
(3)   The birth of Christ at Bethlehem.   (Luke 2:1-20)
(4)   Jesus is presented in the Temple on the fortieth day after his birth.   (Luke 2:22-39)
(5)   The finding of Jesus in the Temple after being lost for three days.   (Luke 2:41-52)

B.   SORROWFUL MYSTERIES (Tuesday and Friday)

(1)   Christ suffers His agony in the Garden.   (Luke 22:39-47)
(2)   Christ is scourged with whips.   (Matt. 27:26)
(3)   Christ is crowned with thorns.   (Matt. 27:27-31)
(4)   Christ carries His Cross.   (Mark 15:20-22)
(5)   The Crucifixion and Death of Christ on the Cross. (Luke 23:23-47)

C.   GLORIOUS MYSTERIES (Wednesday, Saturday & Sunday)

(1)   Jesus arises from the dead on Easter Sunday.   (Matt. 28:1-10)
(2)   Christ ascends into heaven.   (Acts 1:9-11)
(3)   The descent of the Holy Ghost upon the apostles.   (Acts 2:1-8)
(4)   Mary is taken up, body and soul into Heaven.
(5)   Mary is crowned as Queen of Heaven.

CONCLUDING PRAYER:

Hail, Holy Queen, Mother of mercy, our life, our sweetness, and our hope! To thee do we cry, poor banished children of Eve, to thee do we send up our sighs, mournings and weeping in this valley of tears. * Turn then, most gracious advocate, thine eyes of mercy towards us; and after this our exile show unto us the blessed fruit of thy womb Jesus. O clement, O loving, O sweet Virgin Mary.
Pray for us, O holy Mother of God. * That we may be made worthy of the promises of Christ. Amen.

3. The following prayers may be used by the Catholic Lay Leader as a supplement to the Rosary Service or if he wishes he may substitute some of the prayers here listed and combine them with the reading of the Epistle and Gospel of the Sunday from "My Sunday Missal".

ACT OF FAITH O my God, I firmly believe that Thou are one God in three Divine Persons, Father, Son, and Holy Ghost; I believe that Thy Divine Son became man, and died for our sins, and that He will come to judge the living and the dead. I believe these and all the truths which the Holy Catholic Church teaches, because Thou hast revealed them, Who canst neither deceive nor be deceived.

ACT OF HOPE O my God, relying on Thy infinite goodness and promises, I hope to obtain pardon of my sins, the help of Thy grace, and life everlasting, through the merits of Jesus Christ, my Lord and Redeemer.

ACT OF LOVE O my God, I love Thee above all things, with my whole heart and soul, because Thou art all-good and worthy of all love. I love my neighbor as myself for the love of Thee. I forgive all who have injured me, and ask pardon of all whom I have injured.

ACT OF CONTRITION O my God! I am heartily sorry for having offended Thee, and I detest all my sins, because I dread the loss of heaven and the pains of hell, but most of all because I have offended Thee, my God, Who art all good and deserving of all my love. I firmly resolve, with the help of Thy grace, to confess my sins, to do penance, and to amend my life. Amen.

LITANY OF THE SACRED HEART

Lord, have mercy on us.
R. Christ have mercy on us.
Lord, have mercy on us.
R. Christ hear us.
Christ graciously hear us.
God, the Father of Heaven,
R. Have mercy on us. (Response repeated
after each invocation)
God, the Son, Redeemer of the world,
God, the Holy Ghost,
Holy Trinity, one God,
Heart of Jesus, Son of the Eternal Father,
Heart of Jesus, formed by the Holy Ghost
     in the womb of the Virgin Mother,

Heart of Jesus, substantially united to
    the Word of God,
Heart of Jesus, of infinite majesty,
Heart of Jesus, sacred temple of God,
Heart of Jesus, tabernacle of the Most High,
Heart of Jesus, house of God and gate of heaven,
Heart of Jesus, burning furnace of charity,
Heart of Jesus, abode of justice and love,
Heart of Jesus, full of goodness and love,
Heart of Jesus, abyss of all virtues,
Heart of Jesus, most worthy of all praise,
Heart of Jesus, king and centre of all hearts,
Heart of Jesus, in Whom are all the treasures of
    wisdom and knowledge,
Heart of Jesus, in Whom dwells the fullness
    of divinity,
Heart of Jesus, in Whom the Father was well pleased,
Heart of Jesus, of Whose fullness we have all received,
Heart of Jesus, desire of the everlasting hills,
Heart of Jesus, patient and most merciful,
Heart of Jesus, enriching all who invoke Thee,
Heart of Jesus, fountain of life and holiness,
Heart of Jesus, propitation for our sins
Heart of Jesus, loaded down with opprobrium,
Heart of Jesus, bruised for our offenses,
Heart of Jesus, obedient unto death,
Heart of Jesus, pierced with a lance,
Heart of Jesus, source of all consolation,
Heart of Jesus, our life and resurrection,
Heart of Jesus, our peace and reconciliation,
Heart of Jesus, victim for sin,
Heart of Jesus, salvation of those who trust in Thee
Heart of Jesus, hope of those who die in Thee,
Heart of Jesus, delight of all the Saints,

Lamb of God, Who takest away the sins of the world,
R. Spare us, O Lord.
Lamb of God, Who takest away the sins of the world,
R. Graciously hear us, O Lord.
Lamb of God, Who takest away the sins of the world,
R. Have mercy on us.

Jesus, meek and humble of Heart.
R. Make our hearts like unto Thine.

LET US PRAY O Almighty and Eternal God, look upon the
Heart of Thy dearly beloved son, and upon the praise and satisfaction He offers Thee in the name of sinners and for those

who seek Thy mercy; he Thou appeased, and grant us pardon in the name of the same Jesus Christ, Thy Son, Who liveth and reigneth with Thee, in the unity of the Holy Ghost forever and ever. Amen.

PRAYER FOR PURITY

VIRGINAL Mother of God, model and patroness of perfect purity, pray for me with great fervor that I may avoid the illusions and snares of the devil; and may remain innocent and good, through all the temptations and trials of my life on earth. Obtain for me, merciful Mother, a great esteem of innocence and purity, which will make me most pleasing in the eyes of God, and lift me above the corruptions and wickedness of the world. Help me to pray often and fervently for this holy virtue, to avoid the occasions which may threaten or harm it, to shun bad reading, amusements and companionships. Gain for me God's abounding and effective grace, that my eyes may he opened, and my heart strengthened to see and desire all innocence, and to shun and detest all evil.

So may my life he full of manly courage and true self-discipline for the love of Jesus, and may I give my soul to God with untarnished innocence, when I come to die. Thus, may I he preserved from the shameful realization that I have hurt myself and others by sin, and may I deserve to be numbered among the host of the blessed, for all the ages of eternity. This I ardently beseech, through all the merits and prayers of Jesus, through your intercession, my Mother, and that of all God's friends, in time and eternity. With this intention, in union with all the just, in every instant of all time, I helieve in God, all truthful; I hope in Him, all faithful; I love Him, all lovable; and, therefore, I sorrow for all sin. Amen.

PRAYER IN TIME OF TEMPTATION

JESUS, my Eucharistic Savior and Love, stay with me and strengthen me! My holy angel guardian, defend me! All you saints and angels, protect me! I intend and desire, with all my heart, to resist this and every other temptation, instantly and entirely. I will do the holy will of God completely to love and serve Him most faithfully, now and forever. I resist and refuse this temptation for God's love. I recall how short is life, and that eternity knows no end. I know that sin is the only evil, that temptations, faithfully resisted, merit life everlasting. Send me help, therefore, and gain for me grace, abounding and effective, through your merits and prayers, and the intercession of all God's friends, in time and eternity. Through you and with you, for this intention, I believe in God, all truthful; I hope in Him, all faithful; I love Him, all lovable; and, therefore, I sorrow for all sin. Amen.

PRAYER FOR CATHOLIC ACTION

MARY and Joseph, my holy advocates before God, help me to realize and to do always my duty to God and to men. Aid me to choose and to undertake those good works which I can do best, and by which I will most serve and please God, and help others. Save me from wasting energy and time that I might devote to God's service. Make me unselfish, diligent, tactful and kind, in all my work for God's glory. Help me to cooperate effectively with the work of the hierarchy, for the salvation of souls. Give me strength and perseverance, to bring all I undertake to success. Make me docile to those in authority, and gain for me the grace ever to plan and work for the pure love of God, because He is so good, and for the love of my neighbor, for God's sake. I ask it through your merits and prayers, and those of all God's friends, in time and eternity. For this intention, truthful God, I believe in You; faithful God, I hope in You; lovable God, I love You; and, therefore, I sorrow for all sin. Amen.

PRAYER FOR ATONEMENT

MY JESUS, crucified for love of us, scourged and crowned with thorns by our sins, I ardently desire, to the utmost of my powers, to make atonement for all my own sins and those of all Your creatures. I am deeply sorry for all the faults and sins whereby I have offended You, from the first instant of my awakening intelligence, and for all other sins from the beginning of the world. I detest and regret them because they have offended You, who are so good and worthy of my love. I ardently desire and purpose to redouble my efforts to serve and please You hereafter, in atonement and reparation for all sins. I intend in all things to seek Your glory, to do Your will, to accomplish perfectly all that You desire. I yearn and wish that all other creatures may likewise serve and please You perfectly, for Your pure love.

in atonement and satisfaction for all my sins, and for all sins, I offer You Your own holy life, and passion and death. I give to You all the merits and prayers of Mary, of Joseph. and of all Your dear ones, in time and eternity. In union with all the just in every instant of time, and with all my heart, I believe in You, all truthful; I hope in You, all faithful; I love You, all lovable; and, therefore, I sorrow for all sins. Amen.

PRAYER FOR TRUE MANLINESS

MERCIFUL Jesus, my God and my Lord, Savior of my soul,
I ardently beg of You to make me a man, in the truest sense
of that noble word, before God and before men, and at every
instant of my life and death. Fill me, dear Lord, with Your
effective and abounding grace, the fruit of Your sacred Life
and Passion, that I may clearly know, and bravely do, all
that true manliness requires. Make me great in zeal, intelligent and enlightened in faith, firmly to believe all that You
have revealed and Your holy Church teaches. Make me mighty
in hope, full of confidence that You will do all that You have
promised, will help me in temptation and lift me higher and
higher in Your love and service until the end. Above all give
me a great and pure love of Your Divine Goodness, for Your
own sake, and of all my fellows for the love of You. Fill me
with zeal, with love and courage in Your service. Make me
an apostle, to help to spread Your holy Truth, a faithful and
devoted son of Mother Church in all my days and ways. Help
me often to receive You in Holy Communion, to pray to You
with manly fervor, to put Your love and service above all
earthly things. Keep me Yours, in life and death, that I may
glorify You in Heaven, to the utmost of my powers, according
to Your holy Will forever. All this I beseech through Your
own merits and prayers, and the intercession of our Mother
Mary and of St. Joseph, and of all Your friends, in time and
eternity. For this intention, I believe in You, eternal truth:
I hope in You, infinite faithfulness; I love You, adorable lovableness; and, therefore, I sorrow for all sin. Amen.

PRAYER FOR THE POOR SOULS IN PURGATORY

MERCIFUL Jesus, adorable lover of souls, help us and inspire
us to deliver from their sufferings all the poor souls In Pur-
gatory. Bring often to our minds, through Your abounding
and effective graces, the suffering and longing of these poor
souls, waiting on the very threshold of Heaven to be cleansed
of the remains of sin. Move our hearts with love of You and
of souls, so that we may gain the Indulgences, and offer up
many penances and prayers for their speedy release. Let us
not delay, or forget that many of our own dear ones wait in
pitiful anguish for the deliverance we could easily bring. All
this I ardently implore You, through all Your own merits and
prayers, and the prayers and merits of Mary our Mother, of
St. Joseph, and all Your just, In time and eternity. For this
intention, in union with them all forever, I ardently believe In
You, all truthful; I hope in You, all faithful; I love You, all
lovable; and, therefore, I sorrow for all sin. Amen.

PRAYER TO KNOW MYSELF

ETERNAL Spirit of Truth, ever dwelling within me, I humbly
and ardently implore You to give me that self-knowledge which
will best enable me to sorrow for my sins and to love and
serve You perfectly. Strike from my eyes the scales of self-
love and worldliness, that I may see myself as You see me,
a child of God, full of glorious possibilities, yet in great
need of Your help, and in great danger if I yield to my own
evil inclinations. Help me sincerely to acknowledge that whatever I have and am that is good and worthy, is entirely from
You. Arouse in me, by Your effective and abounding grace,
an immense esteem of holiness and a realization of the heights
to which I can rise if only I am true to Your inspirations,
distrusting myself utterly and relying completely on Your power and goodness, let me be filled with courage, faith, hope
and love. Give me joy in suffering, in imitation of my Jesus.
Help me willingly to sacrifice all things to love and serve You
more. Continue in me this priceless grace, past the moment
of my death, so that I may be with You forever in the Kingdom of Your glory. This I beseech You, through the infinite
merits of Jesus, and the intercession of Mary, of Joseph, and
of all Your friends, in time and eternity, while, with an ar-
dent zeal, in union with all the just forever, I believe in You
eternal troth; I hope in You, infinite faithfulness; I love You,
adorable lovableness; and, therefore, I sorrow for all sin.

Amen.

PRAYER FOR PERSONAL LOVE OF CHRIST

JESUS, my Savior, lover of my soul, I ardently implore You
to give me a great and personal love of You. Most manly
and lovable of all our human race, true God and Man, send
Your abounding and effective grace to help me to form in my
mind a just and right conception of Your perfect character and
actions. Open before me the truth of Your teaching, the
beauty of Your life, the splendor of Your perfections, so
that I cannot choose but to love You, with all my heart and
always. With sorrow I say with St. Augustine, "Too late and
too little have I loved You." But now I firmly purpose and
ardently desire to love and imitate You to the utmost of my
powers. "Master lead on, and I will follow Thee to the last
breath, with love and loyalty." But of myself, sweet Jesus,
I am incapable of loving You as I should. Adorable Friend,
draw me to Your friendship. Choose me and take me, to be
Yours forever. To You I dedicate my body and soul, my life
and death, all that I have and am; to be Yours, perfectly and
forever. This I desire, for this I pray, through all Your

own merits and prayers, and the pleadings of Mary and Joseph, and of all Your friends, in time and eternity. For this intention, with all the just forever, I believe in You, all truthfulness; I hope in You, all faithfulness; I love You, all lovableness; and, therefore, I sorrow for all sin. Amen.

PRAYER AGAINST HUMAN RESPECT

MARY and Joseph, pray that I be brave, strong and faithful in resisting temptations to human respect. When my heart sinks at the thought of ridicule and disapproval, may I nevertheless, serve you constantly and openly, and be guided in all things by God's holy Will and His blessed Love. When temptation strikes me, remind me of Jesus crucified, of the shortness of life and the length of eternity. Help me ever to bear witness to my Lord before men, that He may intercede for me with His Father in Heaven. Ask this for me through the merits and prayers of my Jesus, and of our Mother Mary, and of all the friends of God, in time and eternity. To gain this grace, I believe in You, all truthful; I hope in You, all faithful; I love You, all lovable; and, therefore, I sorrow for all sin. Amen.

THE LITANY OF THE BLESSED VIRGIN

Lord, have mercy on us.
R. Christ, have mercy on us.
Lord, have mercy on us.
Christ, hear us.
R. Christ, graciously hear us.
God, the Father of heaven,
R. Have mercy on us.
God, the Son, Redeemer of the world,
R. Have mercy on us.
God, the Holy Ghost,
R. Have mercy on us.
Holy Trinity, one God,
R. Have mercy on us.
Holy Mary,
R. Pray for us (to be repeated
    after each invocation)
Holy Mother of God,
Holy Virgin of virgins,
Mother of Christ,
Mother of divine grace,
Mother most pure,
Mother most chaste,
Mother inviolate,
Mother undefiled,

Mother most amiable,
Mother most admirable,
Mother of good counsel,
Mother of our Creator,
Mother of our Saviour,
Virgin most prudent,
Virgin most venerable,
Virgin most renowned,
Virgin most merciful,
Mirror of justice,
Seat of wisdom,
Cause of our joy,
Spiritual vessel,
Vessel of honor,
Vessel of singular devotion,
Mystical rose,
Tower of David,
Tower of Ivory,
House of Gold,
Ark of the covenant,
Gate of heaven,
Morning star,
Health of the week,
Refuge of sinners
Comforter of the afflicted,
Help of Christians,
Queen of angels,
Queen of patriarchs,
Queen of prophets,
Queen of apostles,
Queen of martyrs,
Queen of confessors,
Queen of virgins,
Queen of all saints,
Queen conceived without original sin,
Queen of the most holy Rosary,
Queen of peace,

Lamb of God, Who takest away the sins of the world,
R.   Spare us, O Lord.
Lamb of God, Who takest away the sins of the world,
R.   Graciously hear us, O Lord.
Lamb of God, who takest away the Sins of the world,
R.   Have mercy on us.

Pray for us, O holy Mother of God.
R.   That we may be made worthy of the promises of Christ.

LET US PRAY. Pour forth, we beseech Thee, O Lord,
Thy grace into our hearts, that we to whom the Incarnation
of Christ Thy Son was made known by the message of an
angel, may by His passion and cross be brought to the
glory of His resurrection. Through the same Christ, our
Lord. Amen.

PRAYER FOR A GOOD DEATH

MARY and Joseph, secure and insure for me a most holy and
happy death. Be with me at my last hour and help me to
make it my best hour. Protect me from all the wiles and
wickedness of the evil one, and strengthen me to love God
with the most pure love and to be sorry for all my sins for
the love of Him. I accept from the Hand of God my death,
with all its circumstances, as He wills, in reparation for all
my sins, and as an act of the pure love of Him. As this
hour comes, may all my trials and sufferings be over, and
may I die a peaceful and happy death, full of faith and hope
and love. I ask it through the prayers and merits of my
Jesus, and through your intercession, our Blessed Mother,
and the prayers of all the friends of God, in time and eternity.
For this, I believe in God, all truthful; I hope in Him, all
faithful; I love Him, all lovable; and, therefore, I sorrow for
all sin. Amen.

4. In Conclusion: The Marine Catholic Lay Leader who is
aboard ship or at some station where the Armed Forces
Hymnal is available will find this an excellent source of prayers and hymns for varying or adding to his Rosary Service
Pages 11 - 76 contain the Stations of the Cross, Novena Prayers, the Litany of the Blessed Virgin and many hymns which
will be familiar to the Marines at the Service. The hymns
particularly, can add beauty and variety to the Service. Pages
37 - 68 of the compact "Song and Service Book" contains a
Catholic section which may also be used. In the temporary
absence of the Catholic Chaplain the Catholic Lay Leader can
put together a meaningful devotional service If he gives the
service thoughtful and prayerful preparation and uses the
above mentioned sources. Such a Rosary Service will indeed,
be spiritually beneficial to himself and to all who participate.

SECTION IX

THE JEWISH LAY LEADER SERVICE

The number of Jewish men in your unit will be small. However their religious and personal needs are no less than they

are for those of other faiths who are greater in number.
Your willingness, dedication, and ability to serve the needs of
these few men of the Jewish faith will bring great glory to the
Lord.

Since there is customarily only one Jewish Chaplain in the
division, you will by necessity function somewhat independently
most of the time. However, the Jewish Chaplain will arrange
for your lay leader training, supply you with needed materials either directly or through your unit chaplain, and maintain as close contact with you as possible. (If necessary,
various materials and services can be obtained by writing
directly to: The National Jewish Welfare Board, 145 East
23rd Street, New York, New York 10010.)

In garrison it is important that you know where and when
Jewish services are held, be familiar with the transportation
which is available to reach them, make sure that this informa-
tion is passed on to the Jewish men in your unit, organize
parties to attend services, and in general, encourage partici-
pation in the total life of the local congregation. You should
also know where the Jewish Chaplain is located, and his
phone number, so that you can make referrals when necessary.
Also, you should make certain that the Jewish Chaplain has
the names of all Jewish men in your unit. Thus he will be
able to maintain personal contact with them and keep them
informed of matters pertaining to the Jewish congregation in
camp. If you have any questions regarding the above, see
your unit chaplain.

It is likely that the only time you will be conducting services
will be when you are in the field. The Sabbath Evening Service which follows may be used. If copies of the "Prayer
Book Abridged For Jewish Personnel" are available, the Sabbath Evening Service on page 127 may be read.

SABBATH EVENING SERVICE

Opening Prayer:

> O Come, let us sing unto the Lord;
> Let us joyfully acclaim the Rock of our salvation.
>
> Let us approach Him with thanksgiving,
> And acclaim Him with songs of praise.
>
> Come, let us worship and bow down;
> Let us bend the knee before the Lord, our Maker,

Sholom Alaychem

Sho-lom a-lay-chem mal-a-chay ha-sho-rays, mal-a-
    chay El-yon,
Mi-meh-lech ma-lechery ha-m'lo-chim, ha-ko-dosh
    bo-ruch hu.

Bo-a-chem l'sho-lom mal-a-chay ha-sho-lom, mal-a-
    chay El-yon.
Mi-meh-lech ma-l'chay ha-m'lo-chim, ha-ko-dosh
    bo-ruch hu.

Bo-r'chu-ni l'sho-lom mal-a-chay ha-sho-lom, mal-a-
    chay El-yon,
Mi -meh -lech ma-l'chay ha-m'lo-chim, ha-ko-dosh
    ho-ruch hu.

Tsay-s'chem l'sho-lom mal-a-chay ha-sho-lom, mal-
    a-chay El-yon,
Mi-meh-lech ma-l'chay ho-m'lo-chim, ha-ko-dosh
    bo-ruch hu

Reader: It is good to give thanks unto the Lord,
             And to sing praises unto Thy name, O
             Most High;

People: To declare Thy loving kindness each morning,
             And Thy faithfulness every night,

Reader: With an instrument of ten strings and the
             lute,
             With sacred music upon the harp.

People: For Thou, O Lord, hast made me rejoice
             in Thy work;
             I will glory in the works of Thy hands.

Reader: How great are Thy deeds, O Lord!
             Thy thoughts are very deep.

People: The ignorant man does not know,
             Nor does the fool understand this -

Reader: The wicked may spring up as the grass,
             And the workers of iniquity may flourish,
             Only to be destroyed forever.

People: But Thou, O Lord, shalt he exalted forever.

Reader: For lo, Thine enemies, O Lord,
            For lo, Thine enemies shall perish;
            All the workers of iniquity shall be scat-
            tered.

People: But Thou dost raise me to high honor;
            I am anointed with fragrant oil.

Reader: Mine eyes have seen the defeat of my foes,
            Mine ears have heard the doom of evil doers
            That rise up against me.

People: The righteous shall flourish like the palm
                tree,
            And grow mighty like a cedar in Lebanon.

Reader: Planted in the house of the Lord,
            They shall flourish in the courts of our God.

People: Even in old age they shall bring forth fruit,
            They shall be full of vigor and strength,

Reader: Declaring that the Lord is just,
            My Rock in whom there is no unrighteousness.

Reader: Bless the Lord who is to be praised.

People: Praised be the Lord who is blessed for
            all eternity.

Reader: Bo-r'-chu es Adonoy ha-m'-vo-roch

People: Bo-ruch Adonoy ha-m' -vo-roch l'o-lom
            vo-ed

Praise be Thou, O Lord our God, Ruler of the universe who
with Thy word bringest on the evening twilight, and with Thy
wisdom openest the gates of the heavens. With understanding
Thou dost order the cycles of time and variest the seasons,
setting the stars in their courses in the sky, according to
Thy will. Thou createst day and night, rolling away the
light before the darkness and the darkness before the light.
By Thy will the day passes into night; the Lord of heavenly
hosts is Thy name. O everliving God, mayest Thou rule
over us forever. Blessed be Thou, O Lord, who bringest
on the evening twilight.

Reader: Hear, O Israel, The Lord Our God, the
            Lord is One.

People: (sing)   Sh'ma Yis-ro-ayl A-do-noy
            Elo-hay-nu A-do-noy E-chod.

Thou shalt love the Lord thy God with all thy heart, with all
thy soul, and with all thy might. And these words which I
command thee this day shall be in thy heart. Thou shalt
teach them diligently unto thy children, speaking of them when
thou sittest in thy house, when thou walkest by the way, when
thou liest down and when thou risest up. And thou shalt bind
them for a sign upon thine hand, and they shall be for front-
lets between thine eyes. And thou shalt write them upon the
doorposts of thy house and upon thy gates.

SILENT PRAYER

Cause us, O Lord our God, to lie down in peace, and raise
us up again, O our King, unto life. Spread over us Thy
tabernacle of peace. Direct us aright through Thine own good
counsel. Save us for Thy name's sake. Be Thou a shield
about us. Remove from us every enemy, pestilence, sword,
famine and sorrow. Help us, O Lord, to resist temptation.
Shelter us with Thy protecting love for Thou art our guardian
and deliverer. Yea, Thou God and King art gracious and
compassionate. Guard our going out and our coming in unto
life and peace, henceforth and forevermore. Yea, do Thou
spread over us the tabernacle of Thy peace. Blessed be Thou,
O Lord, who spreadest the tabernacle of peace over Thy
people Israel, and Jerusalem.

People   The heaven and earth were finished, and all their
and   host. And on the seventh day God had finished His
Reader: work which He had made; and He rested on the
            seventh day from all His work which He had made.
            And God blessed the seventh day, and hallowed it,
            because He rested thereon from all His work which
            God created and made.

Reader: Our God and God of our fathers, accept our rest.
            Sanctify us through Thy commandments, and grant
            our portion in Thy Torah. Give us abundantly of
            Thy goodness and make us rejoice in Thy salvation.
            Purify our hearts to serve Thee in truth. In Thy
            loving favor, O Lord our God, grant that Thy holy
            Sabbath be our joyous heritage, and may Israel who

sanctifies Thy name, rest thereon. Blessed art
Thou, O Lord, who hallowest the Sabbath.

KIDDUSH: Bo-ruch a-toh A-do-noy e-lo-he-nu me-lech
ha-o-lam bo-re pe-ri ha-go-fen.

Ho-ruch a-toh A-do-not e-lo-he-no me-tech
ha-c-lam a-sher ki-d' -sho-un b'mitz -vo-sov
v'-ro-tsoh vo-nu v'-sha-bas ko-d'sho b' -a-ha-voh
uv-ro-tson hin-chi-lo-no, zi-ko-ron l-ma-a-say
v'-re-shis. Ki-hu yom t'-chi-loh l'mik-ro-e
ko-desh, ze-cher li-tsi-as mitz-ro-yim kivo-nu
vo-char-to v'o-so-nu ki-dash-to mi-kol ho-a-mim
vo'-sha-bas kov-sh'-cho b'a-ha-voh uv-ro-tson
hin-chalk -to-no. Bo-ruch a-toh A-do-noy m'-ka-desh
an sha-boss.

ADORATION (People rise and read in unison)

Let us adore the ever-living God, and render 1)raise
onto Him who spread cot the heavens and established
the earth, whose glory is revealed in the heavens
shove and whose greatness is manifest throughout
the world. He is our God; there is none else.

We bow the head in reverence, and worship the
King of kings, the Holy One, praised be He.

Va-a-nach-nu ko-r'-eem o-mish-ta-cha-veem
u-mo-deem, lif-nay me-tech, mal-chay
ham-lo-cheem ha-ko-dosh bo-ruch ho.

People: May the time not be distant, O God, when Thy
name shall be worshiped in all the earth, when
unbelief shall disappear and error be no more.
Fervently we pray that the day may come when all
men shall invoke Thy name, when corruption and
evil shall give way to purity and goodness, when
superstition shall no longer enslave the mind, nor
idolatry blind the eye, when all who dwell on earth
shall know that to Thee alone every knee most bend
and every tongue give homage. O may all, created
in Thine image, recognize that they are brethren,
so that, one in spirit and one in fellowship, they
may be forever united before Thee.
Then shall Thy kingdom be established on earth and
the word of Thine ancient seer be fulfilled:
The Lord will reign forever and ever. On that day
the Lord shall be One and His name shall be One

Reader: And now as we part, let us call to mind those who have finished their earthly course and have been gathered to their eternal home. Wait patiently all ye that mourn, and be ye of good courage, for surely your longing souls shall be satisfied.

(Mourners recite Kaddish at this time)

Yis-ga-dal v'yis-ka -dash sh'may ra-bo, b'o -l'mo di-v'ro chi-r'u-say v'yam-lich ma-l1chu-say, b'cha-yay-chon u-v'yo-may-chon u-v'cha-yay d'chol bays yis-ro-el ba-a-go-lo u-vi-z9man ko-riv, v'i-m'ru O-mayn.

Y'hay sh'may ra-bo m'vo-rach l'o-lam u-l'o-l'may o-l'ma-yo.

Yis-bo-rach, v'yish-ta-bach, v'yis -po-ar, v'yis-ro-mahm, v'yis-na-say, v'yis-ha-dar, v'yis-a-leh, v'yis-ha-lal sh'may d'kud-sho b'rich hu. L'ay-lo min kol bir-cho-so v'shi-ro-so tush-b'cho-so v'ne-che-mo-so, da-a-mi-ron b'o-l'mo v'i-m'ru O-mayn.

Y'hay sh'lo-mo ra-be mm sh'ma-yo v'cha-yim o-lay-nu v'al kol yis-ro-el v'i-m'ru O-mayn.

O-seh sho-lom bim'ro-mov hu ya-a-seh sho-lom o-lay-nu v'al kol yis-ro-el, v'i-m'ru O-mayn.

CLOSING HYMN

Yig-dal E-lo-him chai v'yish-ta-bach,
Nim-tso v'ayn ays el m'tsi-u-so.

E-chod v'ayn yo-chid k'yi-chu-do,
Ne-lom v'gam ayn sof l'ach-du-so.

Ayn lo d'mus ha-guf v'ay-no guf,
Lo na-a-roch ay-lov k'du-sho-so.

Kad-mon l'chol do-vor a-sher niv-ro,
Ri-shon v'ayn ray-shis l'ray-shi-so.

Hino a-don o-lom l'chol no-tsor,
Yo-reh g'du-lo-so u-ma-l'chu-so.

Sheh-fa n'vu-o-so n'so-no,
El an-shay s'gu-lo-so, v'sif-ar-to.

Lo kop b'yis-ro-el k'mo-sheh od,
No-vi, u-ma-bit es t'mu-no-so.

To-ras e-mes no-san l'a-mo ayl,
Al yad n'vi-o ne-e-man bay-so.

Lo ya-cha-lif ho-ayl vllo yo-mir do-so,
L'o-lo-mim llzu-lo-so.

Tso-feh v'yo-day-a s'so-ray-nu,
Ma-bit llsof do-vor blkad-mo-so.

Go-mayl l'ish che-sed k'mif-o-lo,
No-sayn l'ro-sho ra k'rish-o-so.

Yish-lach l'kayts yo-min mlshi-chay-nu,
Lif-dos m'cha-kay kayts y'shu-o-so.

May-sim y'cha-yeh Ayl b'rov chas-do,
Bo-ruch a-day ad shaym tlhi-lo-so.

Kadmon l'chol lo-vor a-sher niv-ro
Ri-shon v'ayn ray-shees l'ray-shee-so

Hi-no A-don o-lom llchol no-tsor
Yo-reh g'du-lo-so u'mul chuso
She-fah n'vu-o-so n'-so-no
El an-shey s'-gu-lo-so V' sif-ar-to

Lo kom b'yi5-ro-ayl, k'mo-she od
No- vee u-mah-beet es t' mu-no-so
To-rus e-mes no-san l'a-mo Ayl
Al yad n'vee-o ne-man bay-so

Lo ya-cha-leef ho-ayl v'-lo-yo-meer do-so
L' o- lo-meem l'zu-lo-so;
Tso-feh v' yo-day-a s'so-ray-nu
Ma-beet l-sof do-vor b' kad-mo-so

Go-mayl l'eesh che-sed k'mif-o-lo,
No-sayn l'ro-sho ra k'rish-o-so;
Yish-lach, l'kayts yo'meen, m'shi-chay nu
Lif-dos mchakeh-ketz y'shu o so.

<u>BENEDICTION</u>:

        May the Lord bless thee and keep thee;
        May the Lord make His countenance to shine upon
           thee and gracious unto thee;
        May the Lord turn His countenance unto thee and
           give thee peace.

NOTE: For other prayers for special occasions; see Prayer
        Book.

SECTION X

<u>EASTERN ORTHODOX LAY LEADER SERVICE</u>

<u>INTRODUCTION</u>

Military situations and necessity do not always permit Eastern
Orthodox personnel to participate in the principle act of Orthodox Worship - - THE DIVINE LITURGY.

There are ships and stations that do not have Eastern Orthodox
Chaplains, as yet. There are times when Orthodox chaplains
may be required to perform temporary, special duties, away
from their ships or stations. And, there are times when dis-
tances do not permit personnel to attend the Divine Liturgy at
a civilian church. At such times, it is advised that appropriate
military permission be obtained for Orthodox personnel to meet
at a designated time and place and organize a PRAYER SERV-
ICE, as set forth in this pamphlet.

                     Chaplain Alexander G. Seniavsky
                     Russian Orthodox Chaplain
                     United States Naval Reserve

A TABLE OF LESSONS OF HOLY SCRIPTURES

To be read at the Lay Leader Service on Sundays, throughout the year. The portions of scripture appointed for the
Epistles and Gospels.

Easter. Liturgy: Epistle: Acts 1:1-8 Gospel: John 1:1-17		
Church Calendar		The Liturgy
	Epistle	Gospel
First week after Easter	Acts 5:12-20	John 20:19-31
Second	Acts 6:1-7	Mark 15:43, 16:8
Third	Acts 9:32-42	John 5:1-15
Fourth	Acts 9:19-26; 29-30	John 6:5-42
Fifth	Acts 16:16-34	John 9:1-38
Sixth	Acts 20:16-18, 28-36	John 7:37-52;8:12
Seventh	Acts 2:1-11	
First week of		
All Saints	Heb. 9:33; 12-2	Matt. 10:32-33,
		37-38; 19:27-30
Second	Horn. 2:10-16	Matt. 4:18-23
Third	Horn. 5:1-10	Matt. 6:22-33
Fourth	Horn. 6:18-23	Matt. 8:5-13
Filth	Horn. 10:1-10	Matt. 8:28; 9:1
Sixth	Horn. 12:6-14	Matt. 9:1-8
Seventh	Horn. 8:1-7	Matt. 9:27-35
Eighth	1 Cur. 1:10-18	Matt. 14:14-22
Ninth	1 Cur. 3:9-17	Matt. 14:22-34
Tenth	1 Cur. 4:9-16	Matt. 18:14-23
Eleventh	1 Cur. 9:2-12	Matt. 18:23-35
Twelfth	1 Cur. 15:1-11	Matt. 19:16-26
Thirteenth	1 Cur. 16:13-24	Matt. 21:33-42
Fourteenth	2 Cur. 1:21; 2:4	Matt. 22:1-14
Fifteenth	2 Cur. 4:6-15	Matt. 22:35-46
Sixteenth	2 Cur. 6:1-10	Matt. 25:14-30
Seventeenth	2 Cur. 6:16; 7:1	Matt. 15:21-28
Eighteenth	2 Cur. 9:6-11	Luke 5:1-11
Nineteenth	2 Cur. 9:31; 12:9	Luke 6:31-36
Twentieth	Gal. 1:11-19	Luke 7:11-16
Twenty-first	Gal. 2:16-20	Luke 8:5-15
Twenty-second	Gal, 6:11-18	Luke 16:19-31
Twenty-third	Eph. 2:4-10	Luke 8:26-39
Twenty-fourth	Eph. 2:14-22	Luke 8:41-56
Twenty-fifth	Eph. 4:1-6	Luke 10:25-37
Twenty-sixth	Eph. 5:9-19	Luke 12:16-21

Easter	Liturgy: Epistle: Acts 1:1-8.	Gospel: John 1:1-17
Church Calendar		**The Liturgy**
	Epistle	Gospel

Church Calendar	Epistle	Gospel
Twenty-seventh	Eph. 6:10-17	Luke 13:10-17
Twenty-eighth	Col. 1:12-18	Luke 14:16-24
Twenty-ninth	Col. 3:4-11	Luke 17:12-19
Thirtieth	Col. 3:12-16	Luke 18:18-27
Thirty-first	1 Tim. 1:15-17	Luke 18:35-43
Thirty-second	1 Tim. 4:9-15	Luke 19:1-10
Sunday before the Ex altation of the Cross	Gal. 6:11-18	John 3:13-17
Sunday after the Ex altation of the Cross	Gal. 2:16-20	Mark 8:34-38; 9:1
Sunday before Christ- mas	Heb. 9:9-10, 17-40	Matt. 1:1-25
Sunday after Christ mas	Gal. 1:11-19	Matt. 2:13-23
Sunday before Epiphany	2 Tim. 4:5-8	Mark 1:1-8
Sunday after Epiphany	Eph. 4:7-13	Matt. 4:12-17
Week of Publican and Pharisee	2 Tim. 3:10-15	Luke 18:10-14
Week of Prodigal Son	1 Cor. 6:12-20	Luke 15:11-32
Meat-fast Week	1 Cor. 8:8; 9:2	Matt. 25:31-46
Cheese-fast Week	Rom. 13:11; 14:4	Matt. 6:14-21
Great Fast (Lent):		
First Week	Heb 9:24-26,32; 12:2	John 1:43-51
Second Week	Heb. 1:10; 2:3; 7:26; 8:2	Mark 2:1-12; John 10:9-16
Third Week	Heb. 4:14; 5:6	Mark 8:34; 9:1
Fourth Week	Heb 6:13-20; Eph. 5:9-19	Mark 9:17-31; Matt. 4:25; 5:12
Fifth Week	Heb. 9:11-14; Gal 3:23-29	Mark 10:32-45; Luke 7:36-50

ORDER OF SERVICE

LEADER: In the name of the Father and of the Son and of
the Holy Spirit, Amen.

CONGREGATION: Glory to Thee, our God, glory to Thee.

LEADER: Heavenly King, the Comforter, Spirit of Truth, Who
art in all places and fillest all things; Treasury of Goodness and Giver of Life; come and abide with us; cleanse
us from every stain, and save our souls, O Lord.

CONGREGATION: Holy God, Holy and Mighty, Holy and Immortal; have mercy upon us.

LEADER: Holy God, Holy and Mighty, Holy and Immortal;
have mercy upon us.

CONGREGATION: Holy God, Holy and Mighty, Holy and Immortal; have mercy upon us.

LEADER: Glory be to the Father and to the Son and to the
Holy Spirit; now and always and forever and ever. Amen.

CONGREGATION: Holy Trinity, have mercy upon us. Lord
cleanse our sins; Master forgive our iniquities; visit and
heal our infirmities, for Thy Name's sake. Lord have
mercy; Lord have mercy; Lord have mercy.

LEADER: Glory be to the Father and to the Son and to the
Holy Spirit; now and always and forever and ever. Amen.

CONGREGATION: Our Father, Who art in heaven, Hallowed
be Thy Name. Thy Kingdom come. Thy will be done, on
earth, as it is in heaven. Give us this day our daily
bread. And forgive us our trespasses, as we forgive those
who trespass against us. And lead us not into temptation,
but deliver us from evil.

LEADER: For Thine is the Kingdom and the Power and the
Glory, of the Father and of the Son and of the Holy Spirit;
now and always and forever and ever.

CONGREGATION: Amen.

LEADER: O Christ our God, Who at all times and at every
hour art worshipped and glorified, in heaven and on earth;

Who art long-suffering, compassionate and merciful; Who
loveth the just and showeth mercy to sinners; Who calleth
all men to salvation through the promise of eternal blessings; Do Thou the same Lord accept our petitions at this
moment, and direct our life toward Thy Commandments.
Make us holy in spirit, pure in body, right in our reason-
ing, clear in our thinking. Deliver us from all affliction,
suffering and pain. Protect us by Thy Holy Angels; so
that, guarded and guided by their company, we may achieve
unity of faith, and attain the vision of Thy surpassing
Glory. For Thou art Blessed unto ages of ages. Amen.

CONGREGATION: Glory be to the Father and to the Son and
to the Holy Spirit.

LEADER: O Lord, be merciful to us, as we trust in Thee;
Visit not Thy wrath upon us beyond measure; And remember not our lawless deeds. But look upon us again with
mercy. And save us from our foes. Thou art our God,
and we Thy people: We are the works of Thy Hands; And
we call upon Thy Name.

CONGREGATION: Now and always and forever and ever.
Amen.

LEADER: O Blessed Mother of God, open the gates of mercy
for us. Our hope is in Thee. May we not go astray; and
may we be delivered from hardship.

CONGREGATION: Amen.

LEADER: Hail Mary, full of Grace; the Lord is with thee.
Blessed art thou among women, and Blessed is the fruit
of thy womb; For thou hast brought forth a Saviour of our
souls.

CONGREGATION: Hail Mary, full of Grace; the Lord is with
thee. Blessed art thou among women, and Blessed is the
fruit of thy womb; For thou hast brought forth a Saviour
of our souls.

LEADER & CONGREGATION: Hail Mary, full of Grace; the
Lord is with thee. Blessed art thou among women and
Blessed is the fruit of thy womb; For thou hast brought
forth a Saviour of our souls.

LEADER: Most glorious Lady, Ever-Virgin Mother of God,
present our prayers to thy Son, our God, entreating Him
to save our souls, through thee.

CONGREGATION: Amen.

LEADER: In peace, let us pray to the Lord.

CONGREGATION: Lord, have mercy.

LEADER: For the peace of the world, and the welfare and
onion of God's Holy Churches, let us pray to the Lord.

CONGREGATION: Lord have mercy.

LEADER: For all Orthodox Patriarchs, Archbishops and
Bishops; the venerable Priesthood, and for all the Christian Clergy and laity, let us pray to the Lord.

CONGREGATION: Lord have mercy.

LEADER: For the President of the United States; and for all
those in Authority over us, let us pray to the Lord.

CONGREGATION: Lord have mercy.

LEADER: For the Officers and Men of our Armed Forces on
land, sea, and in the air, let us pray to the Lord.

CONGREGATION: Lord have mercy.

LEADER: For seasonable weather; for an abundance of the
fruits of the earth; for the sick, travelling and in captiv-
ity or confinement, let us pray to the Lord.

CONGREGATION: Lord have mercy.

LEADER: That He will deliver us from all tribulation, wrath,
danger and necessity, let us pray to the Lord.

CONGREGATION: Lord have mercy.

LEADER: Protect us, have mercy upon us, keep us and save
us, O God, by Thy Grace.

CONGREGATION: Lord have mercy.

LEADER: As we remember our Most Holy, Most Pure, Most
Blessed and Glorious Lady, The Birth-Giver of God and
Ever-Virgin Mary and all the Saints, let us offer ourselves,
and each other, and all our life to Christ, our God.

CONGREGATION: To Thee, O Lord.

LEADER: For unto Thee is due all Glory, Honor and Worship;
to the Father and to the Son and to the Holy Spirit, now
and always and forever and ever.

CONGREGATION: Amen.

LEADER: God standeth in the congregation of the mighty; He
judgeth among the gods.
Praise ye the Lord. Praise God in His sanctuary;
Praise Him in the firmament of His Power.
Let every thing that bath breath praise the Lord.

CONGREGATION: Praise ye Him all His Angels: Praise Him
all His Hosts. To Thee, O God, is due all praise.

LEADER: Glory be to the Holy, Consubstantial, Life-Giving
and Undivided Trinity.

CONGREGATION: Now and always and forever and ever.
Amen. (The congregation is seated)

LEADER: The reading is from the Epistle of......to the
... (reads the appointed lesson from the Book of Acts,
or the Epistles.)

(The (congregation stands)

CONGREGATION: Glory be to God.

LEADER: Let us now attend the reading of the Holy Gospel,
according to Saint..............(reads the Gospel lesson
of the day)

CONGREGATION: Glory to Thee, O Lord, glory to Thee.

LEADER: Let us pray to the Lord.

CONGREGATION: Lord have mercy.

LEADER: O God, our God, Who art praised by the Seraphim
and glorified by the Cherubim, and worshipped by every
heavenly power; Who giveth Wisdom and Understanding to
those who seek Thee and despiseth not sinners, but hath
appointed repentance unto salvation; Who hath enabled us,
Thy humble and unworthy servants, even in this hour to
offer Thee the worship and praise that are due Thee: Do
thou, Merciful Master, forgive our voluntary and involun-
tary transgressions; sanctify our souls and bodies; strength-
en us to serve Thee in holiness all the days of our life:

through the intercession of Thy Blessed Mother and all the Saints.

CONGREGATION: Amen.

LEADER: Blessed is the man that walketh not in the counsel of the ungodly, nor standeth in the way of sinners:

CONGREGATION: Nor sitteth in the seat of the scornful.

LEADER: But His delight is in the law of the Lord.

CONGREGATION: And His law doth he meditate day and night.

LEADER: And he shall be like a tree planted by the rivers of water, that bringeth forth his fruit in his season.

CONGREGATION: His leaf also shall not wither, and whatso- ever he doeth shall prosper.

LEADER: The ungodly are not so:

CONGREGATION: But are like the Chaff which the wind driv eth away.

LEADER: Therefore the ungodly shall nut stand in the judg- ment;

CONGREGATION: Nor sinners in the congregation of the righteous.

LEADER: For the Lord knoweth the way of the righteous:

CONGREGATION: But the way of the ungodly shall perish.

LEADER: Glory he to the Father and the Son and to the Holy Spirit; now and always and forever and ever   Amen.

CONGREGATION: The Father is my Hope; the Son is my Refuge: The Holy Spirit is my Protector. Holy Trinity, have mercy upon us and save us.

LEADER & CONGREGATION: (1) I believe in one God the Father Almighty, Maker of heaven and earth, and of all things visible and invisible;

(2) And in one Lord Jesus Christ the Son of God, the only begotten of the Father before all worlds. Light of Light,

very God of very God, begotten, not made, of one Essence with the Father, through Whom all things were made,

(3) Who for us men and for our salvation came down from heaven, and was incarnate of the Holy Spirit and the Virgin Mary, and was made man;

(4) And was crucified also for us under Pontius Pilate, and suffered and was burled;

(5) And the third day he rose again, according to the Scriptures;

(6) And ascended into heaven, and sitteth at the right hand of the father;

(7) And He shall come again with glory to judge the quick and the dead, and His kingdom shall have no end.

(8) And I believe in the Holy Spirit, the Lord, and Giver of Life, Who proceedeth from the Father, Who with the Father and the Son together is worshipped and glorified, Who spake by the Prophets;

(9) And I believe in One Holy Catholic and Apostolic church.

(10) I acknowledge one Baptism for the remission of sins,

(11) I look for the Resurrection of the dead.

(12) And the life of the world to come   Amen.

LEADER: Let us pray to the Lord.

CONGREGATION: Lord have mercy.

LEADER: O Lord God, Father Almighty and Adorable, though we are denied the spiritual delight of thus approaching and worshipping Thee on this Day, It is just and proper and befitting the majesty of Thy Holiness that we should praise the only existing God, and offer Thee our prayers with a contrite heart and in a spirit of humility.

CONGREGATION: Amen.

LEADER: O Master of Heaven and earth, the Father of our Lord Jesus Christ, our Saviour, Who is the Image of Thy Goodness, the seal of equal type:

CONGREGATION: Reflecting in Himself the Living Word, the true God, our Life, Sanctification and Strength;

LEADER: Through Whom the Holy Spirit was made manifest:

CONGREGATION: The Spirit of Truth, the Gift of Adoption, the Fountain of Holiness.

LEADER: By Whom every rational and intelligent creature is enabled to serve and praise Thee, together with the Angels, Archangels, and all the heavenly Hosts, who go about saying, singing, crying aloud and proclaiming the triumphant hymn:

CONGREGATION: Holy, Holy, Holy, Lord God of Sabaoth; heaven and earth are full of Thy Glory. Hosanna in the Highest; Blessed is He that cometh in the Name of the Lord, Hosanna in the Highest!

LEADER: O Lord God of Hosts, we beseech Thee in this hour to come and dwell in our hearts, unworthy though we be, and make us worthy to approach Thy Majesty. Receive our prayers, as Thou didst accept the gifts of Abel, the Sacrifice of Noah, the Offerings of Abraham, Moses, Aaron, Samuel and all our saintly Forefathers, who have been well-pleasing to Thy Holiness from the beginning of the world. Amen.

CONGREGATION: O Lord, our Good and Merciful God, I acknowledge all my sins, which I have committed each day of my life, in thought, word and deed; in body and soul alike. I am sincerely sorry that I have thus offended Thee and humbly pray Thee: Forgive me, in Thy Mercy, and absolve me of all my transgression. I firmly resolve, with the help of Thy Grace, to turn my way of life away from sin and walk in the path of the righteous and offer praise and glory to Thee, the Father, Son and Holy Spirit. Amen.

LEADER: Let us complete our prayer unto the Lord.

CONGREGATION: Lord have mercy.

LEADER: That the remainder of this day be perfect, holy, peaceful and sinless, let us ask of the Lord.

CONGREGATION: Grant it, O Lord.

LEADER: An angel of peace, a faithful guide, a guardian of our souls and bodies, let us ask of the Lord.

CONGREGATION: Grant it, O Lord.

LEADER: That our Orthodox Archibishops, Bishops, Priests and Deacons and all the Clergy of Thy Church may be preserved in health and long life, rightly dispensing the word of Thy Truth.

CONGREGATION: Grant it, O Lord.

LEADER: That our elected civil authorities, Our Armed Forces, and every city and country may be blessed with a calm and peaceful life in godliness and sanctity.

CONGREGATION: Grant it, O Lord.

LEADER: That all of Thy servants who have gone before us in the hope of resurrection unto life eternal--especially those who have fallen on the fields of struggle for God and Country--may be granted rest in a place of repose and in the blessed sight of Thy Countenance.

CONGREGATION: Remember them eternally, O Lord, and grant this prayer.

LEADER: For Thou art the God of Love and Mercy and unto Thee do we ascribe all glory: to the Father and to the Son and to the Holy Spirit; now and always and forever and ever. Amen.

CONGREGATION: Blessed be the Name of the Lord, from this time forth and forevermore.

LEADER: May the Lord, our God, be merciful unto us, and bless us, and cause His Countenance to shine upon us and give us peace.

CONGREGATION: Through the prayers of Thy Blessed Mother, our Glorious Lady and Ever-Virgin Mary; through the prayers of our Holy Fathers and of all Thy Saints, Lord Jesus Christ, Our God, have mercy upon us and save us.

Amen.

SECTION XI

THE LAY LEADER SERVICES FOR OTHER FAITHS

1. <u>Latter Day Saints</u>

Ministering to Latter Day Saints may be undertaken by those
members of this faith who are trained and cognizant of the
teachings of their church. Aids and materials for private or
public worship and study may be obtained from church headquarters:

> Church Of Jesus Christ Of Latter Day Saints
> The Servicemen's Committee
> 47 East South Temple Street
> Salt lake City, Utah 84111

>   or

> Reorganized Church Of Jesus Christ Of Latter Day Saints
> The Auditorium
> Independence, Missouri

2. <u>Christian Science</u>

Lay Leaders who are to be responsible for ministering to
Christian Science personnel, may obtain materials from:

> Christian Science Activities For Armed Forces
> 107 Falmouth Street
> Boston, Massachusetts 02115

3. <u>Other Faiths</u>: See your chaplain.

SECTION XII

MINISTRY TO THE SICK, WOUNDED, AND DYING

1. <u>Catholic</u>

The Catholic Lay Leader should lead the man who is in danger of dying in repeating this prayer:

> "O My God, I am heartily sorry for having offended
> Thee, and I detest all of my sins because I dread the
> loss of heaven and the pains of Hell, but most of all
> because I have offended Thee My God, who art all

good and deserving of all my love. I firmly resolve
with the help of Thy grace to confess my sins, to do
penance, and to amend my life. Amen."

If time does not permit, or the sick person is incapable of
repeating after you the above prayer in its entirety, then lead
him in repeating at least the following:

"O My God, I am sorry for my sins, because by them
I have offended You. I love You above all things.
With Thy help I will sin no more. Amen."

If a man is dying and a Catholic Priest is unavailable, then
any Christian may administer Baptism in extremis. Take the
following steps:

A.   Ascertain that the man wants to be baptized.

B.   If the indication is affirmative, take ordinary water
      and pour it over his forehead. While pouring the
      water repeat these words: "I Baptize you in the Name
      of the Father and of the Son and of the Holy Ghost."

2. Protestant

A. A Prayer To Be Said For The Sick And Wounded

O Lord, look down from heaven, behold, visit, and relieve
this Thy servant, Look upon him with the eyes of Thy mercy,
give him comfort and sure confidence in Thee, defend him
from the danger of the enemy, and keep him in perpetual
peace and safety; through Jesus Christ our Lord, Amen.

Hear us, almighty and most merciful God and Saviour; extend
Thy accustomed goodness to this Thy servant, who is grieved
with sickness, Sanctify, we beseech Thee, this Thy Fatherly
correction to him; that the sense of his weakness may add
strength to his faith, and seriousness to his repentance; that,
if it shall be to Thy good pleasure to restore him to his
former health, he may lead the residue of his life in Thy
fear, and to Thy glory; or else, give him grace to accept in
faith the salvation won for him by Jesus Christ, so that, after
this painful life is ended, he may dwell with Thee in life
everlasting; through Jesus Christ our Lord. Amen.

B. A Prayer To Be Said When It Appears That A Man Is
Dying

O Father of mercies, and God of all comfort, our only help
in time of need; We fly unto Thee for succor in behalf of
this Thy servant, here lying under Thy hand in great weakness of body. Look graciously upon him, O Lord; and the
more the outward decayeth, strengthen him, we beseech Thee,
so much the more continually with Thy grace and Holy Spirit
in the inner man. Give him unfeigned repentance for all the
errors of his life past, and steadfast faith in Thy Son Jesus,
that his sins may be done away by Thy mercy, and his pardon sealed in Heaven, before he go hence, and be no more
seen. We know, O Lord, that there is no word impossible
with Thee; and that, if Thou wilt, Thou canst even yet raise
him up, and grant him a longer continuance amongst us; yet,
forasmuch as by appearance the time of his dissolution draw-
eth near, so fit and prepare him, we beseech Thee, against
the hour of death, that after his departure hence in peace
and iii Thy favor, his soul may be received into Thine everlasting kingdom; through the merits and mediation of Jesus
Christ Thine only Son. Our Lord and Saviour. Amen.

C. A Prayer To Be Said For A Man At The Point Of Departure

O Almighty God, with whom do live the spirits of just men
made perfect, after they are delivered from their earthly
prisons; We humbly commend the soul of this Thy servant,
our dear brother, into Thy hands, as into the hands of a
faithful Creator, and most merciful Saviour; most humbly beseeching Thee, in the blood of that immaculate Lamb, that
whatsoever defilements it may have contracted in the midst of
this miserable and naughty world, through the lusts of the
flesh, or by the wiles of Satan, being purged and done away
it may be presented pure and without spot before Thee,
through the merits of Jesus Christ Thine only Son our Lord.
Amen.

D. A Prayer To Be Said Over A Man Who Has Expired

If your comrade expires, you may use this Commendation
over him: "Depart, O Christian soul, out of this world, in
the name of God the Father Almighty who created thee. In
the name of Jesus Christ who redeemed thee. In the name
of the Holy Ghost who sanctifies thee. May thy rest be this
day in peace, and thy dwelling place in the Paradise of God."

"O Lord, support us all the day long, until the shadows lengthen and the evening comes, and the busy world is hushed and the fever of life is over, and our work is done. Then in Thy mercy grant (name) a safe lodging, and a Holy rest, and peace at last. Amen."

E. Baptism In Extremis

If a dying man has not been baptized and desires to be, sprinkle a little ordinary water on his head (or another unin-jured portion of his body), saying at the same time these words, "James (use only the Christian name), I baptize you in the name of the Father and of the Son and of the Holy Ghost. Amen."

3. Jewish

Read with the dying man, or for him if he cannot speak, the following:

O Lord, my God and God of my fathers, my destiny is in Thy hands. If it be Thy will, grant me speedy healing of my wounds. But, if not, I shall, with complete trust in Thy wisdom and love, accept whatever may be in store for me. O give me the power to understand that only with Thee is perfect knowledge and that only through Thee does one find boundless happiness and eternal peace. Most sincerely and humbly do I acknowledge my faith in Thee:

Shema Yisroayl Adonoy Elohaynu Adonoy Echod!
Hear, O Israel, the Lord our God the Lord is One!

At the parting of the soul from the body

O MASTER and Lord Almighty, the Father of our Lord
Jesus Christ, Who wiliest that all men should be saved and
cone to the knowledge of the truth; Who desirest not the
death of a sinner, but that he should turn again and live. We
pray Thee and implore Thee, absolve Thou the soul of Thy
servant, (name) from every bond, and free him from every
oath. Remit his transgressions, both of knowledge and of
ignorance, both of deed and of word, which he hath committed
from his youth up, and hath sincerely confessed or bath con
cealed, either through forgetfulness or through shame. For
Thou alone loosest bonds, and restorest the contrite, and art
the hope of the despairing, and canst remit the sins of every
man who putteth his trust in Thee. Yea, Lord who lovest
mankind, command Thou that he be released from the bonds
of the flesh and of sin. Receive Thou in peace the soul of
this Thy servant, (name), and give it rest in that place where
all Thy Saints do dwell; through the grace of Thine Only-be-
gotten Son, our Lord God and Saviour Jesus Christ, with whom
Thou art blessed, and Thine All-Holy, and good and Life-
Creating Spirit: now and ever, and unto ages of ages. Amen.

SECTION XIII

LAY LEADER RESOURCES AND BIBLIOGRAPHY

The following list of compact lay leader aids and resources
is not exhaustive; it is intended only to be representative.
The chaplain will no doubt supply you with some of these for
your use. Items listed in Section IV are not repeated here,

1.   Devotional Guides

      A.   FAMILY ALTAR
            10858 5. Michigan Avenue
            Chicago, Illinois 60628

      B.   THE UPPER ROOM
            1908 Grand Avenue
            Nashville. Tennessee 37212

      C.   THE LINK
            201 Eighth Avenue. South
            Nashville, Tennessee 37203

      D.   THE NATIONAL JEWISH WELFARE HOARD
            145 East 23rd Street
            New York, New York 10010 makes available a
            number of religious tracts and other materials
            for servicemen.

2.   Service Books

      A.   A BOOK OF WORSHIP FOR THE ARMED FORCES
            Presbyterian Church
            Department of Chaplains and Service Personnel
            Nebraska and Van Ness Sts. N. W.
            Washington, D. C. 20016

      B.   ARMED FORCES SERVICE BOOK
            Muhlenberg Press, Philadelphia, Pa.

      C.   A BOOK OF PRAYERS HYMNS AND SERVICES FOR
            THE ARMED FORCES
            National Council Of The Churches in Christ
            297 Fourth Avenue
            New York, New York 10010

      D.   SERVICE PRAYER BOOK
            Armed Services Commission of the Lutheran Church
            Missouri Synod

E.   SERVICE PRAYER BOOK
     Augsburg Publishing House
     Minneapolis, Minnesota

3.   Hymnals

     A.   THE WAYSIDE HYMNAL
          Forward Movement Publications,
          412 Sycamore Street,
          Cincinnati, Ohio 41202

4.   Official Publications

     A.   Armed Forces Hymnal

     B.   Song and Service Hook for Ship and Field

     C.   Catholic Lay Leader Resource Guide
          NavPers 15972

     D.   Protestant Lay Leader Resource Guide
          NavPers 15966